TRACING YOUR SCOTTISH ANCESTRY THROUGH CHURCH AND STATE RECORDS

FAMILY HISTORY FROM PEN & SWORD BOOKS

Birth, Marriage & Death Records
The Family History Web Directory
Tracing British Battalions on the Somme
Tracing Great War Ancestors
Tracing History Through Title Deeds
Tracing Secret Service Ancestors
Tracing the Rifle Volunteers
Tracing Your Air Force Ancestors
Tracing Your Ancestors
Tracing Your Ancestors from 1066 to 1837
Tracing Your Ancestors Through Death Records –
*   Second Edition*
Tracing Your Ancestors through Family
*   Photographs*
Tracing Your Ancestors Through Letters and
*   Personal Writings*
Tracing Your Ancestors Using DNA
Tracing Your Ancestors Using the Census
Tracing Your Ancestors: Cambridgeshire, Essex,
*   Norfolk and Suffolk*
Tracing Your Aristocratic Ancestors
Tracing Your Army Ancestors
Tracing Your Army Ancestors – Third Edition
Tracing Your Birmingham Ancestors
Tracing Your Black Country Ancestors
Tracing Your Boer War Ancestors
Tracing Your British Indian Ancestors
Tracing Your Canal Ancestors
Tracing Your Channel Islands Ancestors
Tracing Your Church of England Ancestors
Tracing Your Criminal Ancestors
Tracing Your Docker Ancestors
Tracing Your East Anglian Ancestors
Tracing Your East End Ancestors
Tracing Your Family History on the Internet
Tracing Your Family History on the Internet –
*   Second Edition*
Tracing Your Female Ancestors
Tracing Your First World War Ancestors
Tracing Your Freemason, Friendly Society and
*   Trade Union Ancestors*
Tracing Your Georgian Ancestors, 1714–1837
Tracing Your Glasgow Ancestors
Tracing Your Great War Ancestors: The Gallipoli
*   Campaign*

Tracing Your Great War Ancestors: The Somme
Tracing Your Great War Ancestors: Ypres
Tracing Your Huguenot Ancestors
Tracing Your Insolvent Ancestors
Tracing Your Irish Family History on the Internet
Tracing Your Irish Family History on the Internet
*   – Second Edition*
Tracing Your Jewish Ancestors
Tracing Your Jewish Ancestors – Second Edition
Tracing Your Labour Movement Ancestors
Tracing Your Legal Ancestors
Tracing Your Liverpool Ancestors
Tracing Your Liverpool Ancestors – Second Edition
Tracing Your London Ancestors
Tracing Your Medical Ancestors
Tracing Your Merchant Navy Ancestors
Tracing Your Northern Ancestors
Tracing Your Northern Irish Ancestors
Tracing Your Northern Irish Ancestors – Second
*   Edition*
Tracing Your Oxfordshire Ancestors
Tracing Your Pauper Ancestors
Tracing Your Police Ancestors
Tracing Your Potteries Ancestors
Tracing Your Pre-Victorian Ancestors
Tracing Your Prisoner of War Ancestors: The First
*   World War*
Tracing Your Railway Ancestors
Tracing Your Roman Catholic Ancestors
Tracing Your Royal Marine Ancestors
Tracing Your Rural Ancestors
Tracing Your Scottish Ancestors
Tracing Your Second World War Ancestors
Tracing Your Servant Ancestors
Tracing Your Service Women Ancestors
Tracing Your Shipbuilding Ancestors
Tracing Your Tank Ancestors
Tracing Your Textile Ancestors
Tracing Your Twentieth-Century Ancestors
Tracing Your Welsh Ancestors
Tracing Your West Country Ancestors
Tracing Your Yorkshire Ancestors
Writing Your Family History
Your Irish Ancestors

TRACING YOUR SCOTTISH ANCESTRY THROUGH CHURCH AND STATE RECORDS

A Guide for Family Historians

CHRIS PATON

Pen & Sword
FAMILY HISTORY

First published in Great Britain in 2019 by
PEN AND SWORD FAMILY HISTORY
An imprint of
Pen & Sword Books Ltd
Yorkshire – Philadelphia

ISBN 978 1 52676 842 1

Printed and bound in the UK by TJ International Ltd,
Padstow, Cornwall.

Pen & Sword Books Limited incorporates the imprints of Atlas,
Archaeology, Aviation, Discovery, Family History, Fiction, History,
Maritime, Military, Military Classics, Politics, Select, Transport,
True Crime, Air World, Frontline Publishing, Leo Cooper, Remember
When, Seaforth Publishing, The Praetorian Press, Wharncliffe
Local History, Wharncliffe Transport, Wharncliffe True Crime
and White Owl.

For a complete list of Pen & Sword titles please contact

PEN & SWORD BOOKS LIMITED
47 Church Street, Barnsley, South Yorkshire, S70 2AS, England
E-mail: enquiries@pen-and-sword.co.uk
Website: www.pen-and-sword.co.uk

Or

PEN AND SWORD BOOKS
1950 Lawrence Rd, Havertown, PA 19083, USA
E-mail: Uspen-and-sword@casematepublishers.com
Website: www.penandswordbooks.com

CONTENTS

INTRODUCTION

Genealogists and family historians seek materials within archives which document the very existence of the people we are hoping to learn about from our ancestral pursuits. In Scotland, our forebears were thankfully great advocates of a quill and ink, and as a consequence have left behind a wealth of material to help us on our way.

For centuries Scotland was an independent nation, before economic pressures and issues surrounding the royal succession led to a political union with England and Wales in 1707, creating a relationship which has at times been cautious and challenged by political circumstances. While the union led to a more homogeneous approach to worldwide affairs, as the British Empire flourished, within Britain itself Scotland remained virtually independent from its partners in many ways.

Following the union, Scotland retained its own legal system, which has been heavily influenced by Roman Law and by the feudal form of land tenure, maintained for centuries long after being abandoned by the rest of Britain. Scotland kept its own state church, one that differed markedly from its Anglican equivalent, but which for much of its existence fought with itself over the issue of control between its flock and its patrons. Scotland also kept its own education system, which in itself has seen many challenges, not least through the rapidly changing demographics of the Scottish population caused by the Industrial Revolution, as well as the aftermath of the Irish Famine in the mid-nineteenth century.

The idea for this book emerged from a series of short guides that I initially produced for an Australian company called Unlock the Past, which sought to explore a variety of Scottish topics from a Scots-based perspective. To understand Scotland's records is not as straightforward as applying what you already know from other jurisdictions and hoping for the best. Scotland's records have their own legal language, and their own reason for existing. In some cases, such as with the land-based sasine records, they are simply not replicated anywhere else in the world, while many records, such as our parish and civil registration records, provide a mixture of similarities and differences to other countries' holdings in equal measure.

In this book, I will look at many of the most common records used by family historians in Scotland, ranging from the vital records kept by the state and the various churches, censuses and other records noting where people resided at any one time, registers of land ownership and inheritance, and records of law and order.

Through each topic I will discuss a variety of offerings both online and offline, and explain much of the legal background to their creation, the language that they use, and the concepts they were designed to record. It is hoped that in understanding the nature of the records, the reader will become better equipped to find them, to wrestle with them, and to ultimately emerge as the victor in their Caledonian pursuits.

Finally, a huge thank you to Rupert Harding, Amy Jordan, Pamela Covey and the team at Pen and Sword, to Alan Phillips, Rosemary Kopittke and Kirsty Wilkinson, and to my wife and sons. A special thanks also to the Patons, MacFarlanes, MacGillivrays, McEwans, Munros, Camerons, Frasers, Bennets, Bruces, Galletlys, Grahams, Hendersons, Rogers, Leitchs, Lambs, Patersons, Shepherds, Hays, Straittons and Broughs. All Scots who came before me and gave me something to write about.

Alba gu bràth.

GLOSSARY

CPRs	Catholic Parish Registers
GROS	General Register Office for Scotland
IGI	International Genealogical Index (FamilySearch)
LDS	Latter-day Saints (FamilySearch)
NLS	National Library of Scotland
NRAS	National Register of Archives for Scotland
NRS	National Records of Scotland
OPRs	Old Parish Registers (Church of Scotland)
RNE	Register of Neglected Entries
SCA	Scottish Catholic Archives
SCAN	Scottish Archive Network

Chapter 1

RESEARCH RESOURCES

There are many repositories that hold records across Scotland, and many resources that can help to get the best out of them in terms of understanding their content, whether through the language used within them or the handwriting in which they are recorded.

The following institutions and tools will be referred to repeatedly throughout this book.

National Records of Scotland
HM General Register House, 2 Princes Street, Edinburgh EH1 3YY
www.nrscotland.gov.uk
Tel: +44 (0)131 334 0380

The National Records of Scotland (NRS) is the national archive for Scotland, formed in April 2011 by a merger of the National Archives of Scotland and the General Register Office for Scotland (GROS). An overview of Scottish Government records held by the NRS from post-1707 is available at **www.nrscotland.gov.uk/research/guides/scottish-government-records-after-1707**

The archive's website does not host digitized records, but does provide an impressive catalogue and detailed research guides. The Historic Search Room provides digital access to several collections through its Virtual Volumes computer system, with printing available, and it is possible to photograph many records for personal use, although the records catalogued as Gifts and Deposits (GD) are an exception to this.

Many digitized records from the NRS, such as tax records and Ordnance Survey Name Books, are freely available on the ScotlandsPlaces website at **https://scotlandsplaces.gov.uk**, a project run in partnership with the National Library of Scotland and Historic Environment Scotland.

ScotlandsPeople Centre

2 Princes Street, Edinburgh EH1 3YY

www.nrscotland.gov.uk/research/visit-us/scotlandspeople-centre

Tel: +44 (0)131 314 4300

The ScotlandsPeople Centre is a joint venture between the NRS and the Court of the Lord Lyon, and is based on the ground floors of both General Register House and New Register House on Princes Street in Edinburgh. For a daily fee of £15, it offers unlimited access to digitized civil registration records for post-1855 births, marriages and deaths, pre-1855 parish records from the Church of Scotland and nonconformist Presbyterian churches, additional registers for the Roman Catholic Church, census records (1841–1911), wills and testaments from 1513, valuation rolls from 1855, and the *Public Register of All Arms and Bearings in Scotland* from 1672 to 1916.

Many of these records can also be purchased from its online website at **www.scotlandspeople.gov.uk**. Your user account at home can be used in the centre's database, but more recent records consulted at the centre cannot be viewed at home, with the online version of the site imposing closure periods for certain records categories for privacy reasons. The

The ScotlandsPeople Centre and the National Records of Scotland are both based within General Register House in Edinburgh.

centre also has an onsite library, with many useful resources, and a café.

Access to the ScotlandsPeople Centre's complete version of the database is also permitted in other regional centres across Scotland, based in Glasgow, Kilmarnock, Hawick, Alloa and Inverness, for the same statutory daily fee. Further details are available at **www.nrscotland.gov. uk/research/local-family-history-centres**

Court of the Lord Lyon
HM New Register House, Edinburgh EH1 3YT
www.courtofthelordlyon.scot
Tel: +44 (0)131 556 7255

The Court of the Lord Lyon is Scotland's heraldic authority and responsible for the maintenance of the *Public Register of All Arms and Bearings in Scotland*, available on the ScotlandsPeople website. As a working court of the Crown, its role and records are further discussed on p.149.

National Library of Scotland
George IV Bridge, Edinburgh EH1 1EW
www.nls.uk
Tel: +44 (0)131 623 3700

The National Library of Scotland (NLS) is Scotland's national library, with books, rare manuscripts, audio-visual materials and maps among its many impressive holdings.

The NLS website hosts many important digitized record sets, including maps, gazetteers and Post Office directories. The site also has a Digital Gallery area at **https://digital.nls.uk/gallery** with additional fascinating projects such as Scottish History in Print, which hosts various transcribed historic publications, and two volumes of MacFarlane's *Genealogical Collections Concerning Families in Scotland 1750–1751*. The library also has a dedicated platform on the Internet Archive at **https://archive.org/ details.nationallibraryofscotland,** which hosts many additional digitized resources not found on its own website.

Historic Environment Scotland
John Sinclair House, 16 Bernard Terrace, Edinburgh EH8 9NX
www.historicenvironment.scot
Tel: +44 (0)131 662 1456

Historic Environment Scotland (HES) is an environmental agency formed in 2015 by the merger of the Royal Commission on the Ancient and Historical Monuments of Scotland and Historic Scotland.

HES offers a search room for visitors where you can access original archive and collections material, while its Canmore database at **https://canmore.org.uk** also provides information for much of Scotland's archaeology, buildings, industrial and maritime heritage.

Registers of Scotland

Edinburgh: Meadowbank House, 153 London Road, Edinburgh EH8 7AU
Glasgow: St Vincent Plaza, 319 St Vincent Street, Glasgow G2 5LP
www.ros.gov.uk
Tel: 0800 169 9391

Registers of Scotland is the Scottish Government's department responsible for keeping public registers of land, property and other legal documents in Scotland. It manages the Land Register of Scotland and the post-1868 General Register of Sasines (with earlier sasines registers kept at the NRS). A brief history of property registration in Scotland is available on its website at **www.ros.gov.uk/about/what-we-do/our-history**

It is possible to visit either of the agency's two offices to carry out research. An online enquiry service is also available.

Scottish Council on Archives
www.scottisharchives.org.uk

The SCA provides support for many archives found across Scotland, including local county archives, university archives, community archives, health archives and business collections.

To locate contact details for such archives, visit the SCA's Scottish Archives map at **www.scottisharchives.org.uk/explore/scottish-archives-map**. The Archives Hub site may also help at **https://archiveshub.jisc.ac.uk**

Scottish Archive Network
www.scan.org.uk

If an archive does not have its own dedicated online catalogue, it may have some collections descriptions available on the Scottish Archive Network (SCAN) database at **https://catalogue.nrscotland.gov.uk/scancatalogue/welcome.aspx**, which is maintained by the NRS.

The SCAN website also hosts useful research tools and glossaries which can help users to understand the context of many records offerings.

National Register of Archives for Scotland
https://catalogue.nrscotland.gov.uk/nrasregister/welcome.aspx

Established in 1946, the National Register of Archives for Scotland (NRAS) is today managed by the NRS and documents significant collections held in private hands, including estate papers, law firms and business collections.

FamilySearch Family History Centres
Various locations worldwide
www.familysearch.org

The Church of Jesus Christ of Latter-day Saints runs a series of family history centres across Scotland and worldwide which can be located through its website at **www.familysearch.org/locations/centerlocator?cid=lihp-fhlc-5508**. The Church has gone to extraordinary lengths to secure photographs and digitized copies of records from around the world, including parish records, land records, maps and more. To locate such holdings, consult the catalogue on its website. FamilySearch also hosts indexes to many records, including its International Genealogical Index (IGI), which includes Scottish church and state records for births and baptisms, and marriages.

Scottish Association of Family History Societies
www.safhs.org.uk

SAFHS is the umbrella body for most family history societies in Scotland. Its website provides contact details for member groups, and some useful online finding aids.

Commercial Websites
In addition to ScotlandsPeople, several other commercial websites exist which offer finding aids for Scottish church and state records. The following are some of the most useful:

Scottish Indexes
Scottish Indexes (**www.scottishindexes.com**) offers a finding aid to many NRS holdings, including mental health records, its criminal

Scottish Indexes provides many handy finding aids for materials at the National Records of Scotland.

records database, Scottish Paternity Index, Register of Deeds, Register of Sasines, Kelso Dispensary Patient Registers, non-OPR-based births/ baptisms, banns/marriages, and deaths/burials, and census holdings.

Old Scottish Genealogy & Family History

Among its finding aids, Old Scottish (**www.oldscottish.com**) has indexes for asylum patients, Poor Law appeals, paternity and illegitimacy records, anatomy registers, communion rolls, baptisms and kirk session records.

Ancestry

Ancestry (**www.ancestry.co.uk**) is an American subscription-based site which offers digitized collections of state records as held by The National Archives (TNA) in England (for example, British military records, and passenger records as held by the Board of Trade), but also some records for Scotland, as sourced from Scottish-based archives.

FindmyPast

As with Ancestry, FindmyPast (**www.findmypast.co.uk**) also hosts many collections from TNA in England.

Handwriting

Understanding older forms of handwriting can be a serious problem for the inexperienced, particularly the case with Secretary Hand, a highly-stylized form used commonly until the late-eighteenth century, with many letters seemingly completely unrelated to their modern equivalent. To get to grips with its basics, the NRS has a Scottish Handwriting website at **www.scottishhandwriting.com** offering a series of free tutorials that should soon bring you up to speed. For illegible handwriting you may need to look at other entries on the page to try to understand the style and convention of letters and words used.

Note that you may also find words written as 'ys', 'yt' and 'yr', meaning 'this', 'that' and 'there'. The first letter of these words is not actually a 'y', but an old obsolete letter known as a 'thorn', which looked more like a letter 'p' with both a long ascending and descending stroke beside the loop. In modern type the letter 'y' in English is often used as a convenient way to transcribe the old letter, but it is in fact pronounced as a 'th', which is how words formally spelled with a thorn have been standardized today.

Another letter missing today from Scots use is the 'yogh', which looked a little like the number '3'. In modern spelling the letter 'z' has replaced it. Examples can be found in words such as the names Menzies and Dalziel, which were not historically pronounced as 'men-zees' and 'dal-zeel' but as 'ming-iss' and 'dee-yell', and are still pronounced as such by many people today. The yogh was a letter pronounced historically as a thin 'gh' or a 'y'.

Languages
Much of what you will read in historical documents may be written in Scots, not in English. Scots is not a dialect of English as many think, but a separate, but closely-related Germanic language. If there is a word that

A bilingual inscription in Gaelic and English at Culloden Visitor Centre, near Inverness.

you can easily read but have absolutely no idea about its meaning, try consulting the Dictionary of the Scots Language at **www.dsl.ac.uk**

Scotland's other historic language is Gaelic (Gàidhlig), which may also pop up within records. A handy online translation tool is Google Translate, available at **https://translate.google.co.uk**

Many documents were also written in Latin. Google Translate can also help with this, but a useful guide to help with Latinized legalisms is the *Student's Glossary of Scottish Legal Terms* (W. Green & Sons Ltd, 1946), as well as the Scottish Law Online website at **www.scottishlaw.org.uk/ lawscotland/abscotslawland.html**. Peter Gouldesbrough's *Formulary of Old Scots Documents* (Stair Society, 1985) is a further invaluable aid.

Chapter 2

CIVIL REGISTRATION

The civil registration of births, marriages and deaths commenced in Scotland in January 1855. As with many areas of Scottish genealogy, the law surrounding registration varies considerably with the rest of the United Kingdom.

The main civil registration records for births, marriages and deaths are available on the ScotlandsPeople platform (p.2), with additional records available for consultation at the ScotlandsPeople Centre in Edinburgh. In this chapter we will discuss what is contained in such records, and the legal requirements of registration. A very useful source for those wishing to learn more about such records is G.T. Bisset Smith's invaluable and essential guide, *Vital Registration: A Manual of the Law and Practice concerning the Registration of Births, Deaths and Marriages* (William Green and Sons, 1907).

Establishment of Civil Registration

Prior to 1855, the Church of Scotland was the body tasked with keeping records of baptisms, marriages and banns, and deaths and burials (see Chapter 3). For many years, however, it had been recognized that the Kirk was failing to maintain a sufficiently high standard of record-keeping, as factors conspired against its effectiveness. Not only was the parochial system falling apart as the Industrial Revolution rapidly transformed the country, but tensions within the Kirk itself, particularly over the issue of patronage, repeatedly ripped it apart through a series of schisms, most notably in the Great Disruption of 1843 (p.35).

A useful guide from 1849 recording the condition of many parish registers is *Scottish Parochial Registers: Memoranda of the State of the Parochial Registers of Scotland* by William B. Turnbull, drawn up to impress upon the state the need for a national system of civil registration. This has been digitized and can be accessed on Google Books at **https://tinyurl. com/4swm4zx** or via the Internet Archive at **https://archive.org/details/ scottishparochia00turnuoft**. Although incomplete in that some parishes did not respond to my requests for information, it is still a useful resource for understanding why many records did not in fact survive.

The role of the Registrar General for Scotland and the General Register Office for Scotland (GROS) were both established by the Registration of Births, Deaths and Marriages (Scotland) Act 1854 (see **https://tinyurl.com/48b8kxp**). The first building occupied by the GROS was the Edinburgh-based General Register House, now host to the ScotlandsPeople Centre and the National Records of Scotland, with the agency soon relocating to the adjacent New Register House in 1863. Unlike the prior introduction of civil registration in England and Wales in July 1837, it became compulsory in Scotland to register vital record events from the moment the relevant legislation became active in January 1855. The act of registration itself was free in most cases.

The country was divided from 1855 into 1,027 registration districts, mostly following the boundaries of the existent Church of Scotland parishes, although this rose to 1,082 by 1910. A breakdown of these districts, and how they have changed over the years, is available at **https:// tinyurl.com/ScottishRegistrationDistricts**. In many cases the original registrars were schoolmasters, session clerks and Poor Law inspectors. The earliest registers vary in the quality of what was recorded, but with annual inspections soon implemented by the GROS, it did not take long for the system to shape up. Two copies of the registers were kept: one for local use, the other for the centralized GROS in Edinburgh.

From 1855 to the present day various Acts of Parliament have been enacted impacting on the subsequent work of the GROS. For a comprehensive list, and a more detailed history of the GROS' creation, consult **https://tinyurl.com/GROShistory**

Registration of Births
The law required that a birth in Scotland had to be registered within twenty-one days, upon penalty of a twenty shillings fine. This was to be done in the area where the father was deemed to be resident or 'domiciled' in cases of legitimate births, or in that of the mother when the child was deemed illegitimate (p.13), the exception being for female domestic servants, whose district of domicile could be reckoned as that of her parents. The births were recorded in the Registry Books using the form of a Schedule A document which was appended to the 1854 Registration Act.

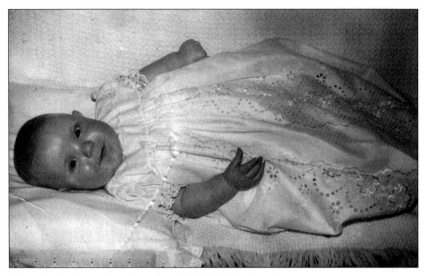

The author's christening photo from 1971 in Helensburgh.

If the baby was born in a different Scottish district to that where the parent usually resided, the birth could be registered in the birth district, but within eight days a copy then had to be sent by the registrar to the registration office within the district of the parents' residence and re-registered. For this reason, you might come across two entries for the same birth on ScotlandsPeople. This only applied in Scotland, so if the normal family residence was perhaps in England or Ireland, the birth only had to be registered within the Scottish district where it occurred. This requirement to re-register births in a separate district was removed in 1934.

It was illegal for a registrar to record a birth himself without a qualified informant present, who had to be at least 14 years of age. The following were considered suitable candidates for the role:

i) A parent or parents was the preferred option, as they would be best placed to pass on the required details. It was advised that a copy of a marriage extract should be brought along as evidence when the birth was registered. In practice, the father most often acted as the informant.

ii) A person in charge of the child; i.e. a legally appointed guardian.

iii) The occupier of the house where the birth occurred. Alternatively, an authority in charge of a prison, a house of correction, a poorhouse, a hospital, an asylum or a charitable institution.

iv) A nurse who had been in attendance at the birth.

Failing this, 'any other person having knowledge of the particulars' could be permitted to act as an informant. When a birth was registered, the informant was given a copy of the entry made into the register that he or she had signed.

If the birth was not registered within twenty-one days, the registrar would contact the person with primary care for the child, either by letter or in person, to compel them to turn up to carry out the procedure. Registrars were permitted to do so twice, before a three-month period had expired. If the parents or primary carers had left the registration district, it was possible for a nurse or a doctor to act as the informant instead.

If after three months there was still no registration, the county sheriff (p.132) would be informed, as would the local procurator fiscal (p.134). The sheriff would issue a warrant compelling attendance, while the fiscal would commence prosecution proceedings. The following is an example of such a case as reported in the *Dundee Courier* on 4 July 1855:

WARNING – REGISTRATION ACT

On Monday, Robert Mann, agricultural labourer, West Newbigging, New Vigeans, appeared before Mr Sheriff Henderson, to answer to a complaint preferred against him at the instance of the Procurator Fiscal, for a contravention of the new Registration Act, he having failed within the statutory period of twenty-one days to give the requisite information to the registrar of his district, relative to the birth of a female child of which his wife was delivered on 14th May last, whereby he had incurred a penalty not exceeding twenty shillings. The Sheriff convicted him on his confession, and adjudged him to pay a fine of ten shillings in name of modified penalty, besides two pounds ten shillings of expenses.

At this stage, the parent or carer would have to make a subsequent declaration about the child's birth, which the sheriff would then allow to be recorded in the birth register, although in such cases a district examiner was required to formally sign the register entry rather than a registrar. Any attempt to register a birth after three months by a parent or guardian, without the authority of a sheriff, incurred a fine of up to £5.

It was possible within six months of registration to make an amendment to the name recorded in the register. If this was done at baptism, the officiating minister was to fill out a simple declaration form (Schedule D as appended to the 1854 Registration Act), detailing the child's name, which the parent or guardian would then convey to the registrar. A fee of a shilling was charged to have the correction noted within the Register of Corrected Entries (RCE, p.31). Changes requested after six months could only be made with a sheriff's permission.

Illegitimacy

If a child was illegitimate, its birth was normally registered by the mother. The father's name, in such circumstances, could only be included in the birth register if he attended the registration alongside the child's mother, and with her agreement. In such cases, the child could be recorded with the father's surname; if the father was not in attendance, the child had to be recorded with the mother's surname. Prior to 1919, the word 'illegitimate' was then written beneath the child's name in the first column. It should be noted that any child born to a couple who had married irregularly (p.22) was deemed legitimate, even if such a marriage was never registered.

It was long recognized in Scotland that following the subsequent marriage of an illegitimate child's parents, the child could be legitimized but only if the parents had been free to marry at the time when it was conceived (i.e. not born from an adulterous affair). In such a case, this could be noted within the Register of Corrected Entries, once the registrar was shown the marriage certificate, with a reference added to the left margin of the birth register entry. You may also find the child's birth registered for a second time following such a marriage, with its new surname.

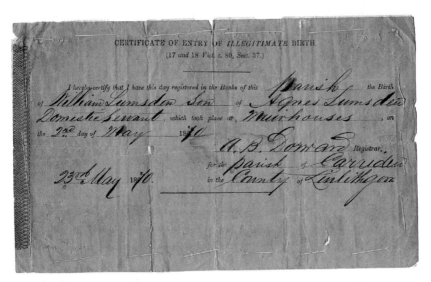

A 'Certificate of Entry of Illegitimate Birth' from 1870 for William Lumsden, signed by the registrar of Carriden. (By kind permission of Kirsty Wilkinson)

However, this was only possible if the father had previously acknowledged paternity. If not, he would be first required to petition the sheriff for a warrant to acknowledge him as the father, with an inquiry then held into the matter. If there were no objections, the warrant would be granted, and in conjunction with a copy of the marriage certificate as evidence, the registrar could then record the correction. Of course, not every father acknowledged paternity, in which case a court action may have been brought against him.

An index for some 33,000 sheriff court paternity extract decrees from 1855 to 1900 is available online through Old Scottish, with earlier records from 1830 onwards available on Scottish Indexes for counties south of the Forth and Clyde, as well as for Aberdeen Sheriff Court. Scottish Indexes also offers an online research guide entitled 'Tracing Your Illegitimate Ancestors in the Sheriff Court Records'.

Locating Birth Records

Scottish births were recorded in the Registry Books using a Schedule A form, as defined by the 1854 Registration Act and subsequently amended. The information required was as follows:

- The name of the child. If illegitimate, this was noted under the child's name, a practice not discontinued until 1919
- The date and time of birth, and where born: street, number and parish. If the child was a twin, the word 'twin' was to be written in the outer margin of the entry, although this was not always done. For the place of birth, the name of the parish had to be recorded if there was more than one within the relevant registration district.
- The sex of the child, noted as 'M' or 'F'
- The father's name and occupation. If a craftsman, he was to be recorded as an 'apprentice', 'journeyman' or 'master'. If deceased, this was also noted.
- The mother's name, including maiden surname and any previous married surnames (see p.26)
- The date and parish location of the parents' marriage (this was not included in entries from 1856 to 1860)
- The name of the informant, his or her residence if not at the place of birth, and whether present at the event
- The date and place of registration, and the registrar's name.

For the year 1855 only, the following additional details were also recorded:

- The father's age and birthplace
- The number of children produced by the parents, and how many of those were still alive at the time of registration
- The mother's age and birthplace.

Images of historic records, older than 100 years, are available on the online ScotlandsPeople website, with indexes available for more recent records. In the records for the year 1855, and from 1929 onwards, the mother's maiden name is noted; however, for the online version of the database, the mother's maiden name is not provided in the index for records within the last 100 years for privacy purposes. At the ScotlandsPeople Centre (and equivalent centres), the images are available for records within this online closure period.

Scottish statutory birth registrations from 1855 to 1874 are also included with the FamilySearch website collection entitled 'Scotland Births and Baptisms 1564–1950', and within the site's IGI (p.5). This notes the parents' names, the child's name, the date of birth and location where registered.

Minor Records of Births
The GROS did not just record vital events from within Scotland, but also those concerned with Scots residing or working overseas in certain capacities. The records are accessible via ScotlandsPeople.

Only one category for such births was the responsibility of the GROS upon its creation in 1855. The details of any child born at sea on a British vessel to a Scottish parent were to be recorded by the captain of the vessel in his log book. Upon arrival at any UK port he was then to forward the details by post to the Registrar General in Edinburgh, who would duly record the information in the Marine Register. Within three days the Registrar General was also required to send a copy of such details to the local registrar of the parish in which the parents were usually domiciled, if known.

The responsibility for births at sea on merchant vessels was formally transferred in 1874 to a new UK-based authority, as per Section 37 of the Registration of Births and Deaths Act 1874 (see **www.legislation. gov.uk/ukpga/Vict/37-38/88/enacted**). Captains of merchant vessels were now required to send such information to the Registrar General of Shipping and Seamen, who had to regularly notify the GROS of any children born to Scots at sea. An exception concerned children born on Royal Navy ships, for whom the Registrar General for Scotland was still to be notified directly. The Marine Register returns are accessible within the 'Minor Records' series on the respective ScotlandsPeople databases.

Additional 'Minor Records' databases include:

- 'Foreign Returns' (1860–1965), listing details of the births of children born to Scots in foreign countries that were not British colonies or dependencies, which have been certified by a British consul in the relevant country and transmitted within twelve months of such certification to Edinburgh. Births in a colony were registered in the colony itself.
- 'Consular Returns' (from 1914), containing birth registrations by British consuls relating to persons of Scottish descent.
- 'High Commission Returns' (from 1964), containing details of children born of Scottish descent in various Commonwealth countries.
- 'Service Returns' (from 1881), including Army Returns of births of Scottish persons at military stations abroad (1881–1959) and Service Departments Registers (from 1959) incorporating births outside the United Kingdom of children of Scottish residents serving in or employed by HM forces.
- 'Air Register' (from 1948) for a child for whom at least one parent was a Scottish resident and born overseas in a British-registered aircraft.

Further information on these is available via the NRS Minor Records of Births, Deaths and Marriages Overseas guide at **www.nrscotland.gov. uk/research/guides/birth-death-and-marriage-records/minor-records**

Stillbirths

A Register of Stillbirths was not created in Scotland until 1939. Upon implementation, the period within which such an event was to be registered was set at twenty-one days; still the case today. Either parent can register the stillbirth; however, a father can only be named on a stillbirth entry if present at the time of the registration with the mother, if the court has found that he is the father, or if both parents sign declaration forms to that effect (available from the registrar). Only parents can request copies of such records upon written application to the NRS, following payment of the appropriate fee. The records are not available on ScotlandsPeople.

Prior to 1939, stillborn children were not registered by law. A child was deemed stillborn if it was unable to breathe for itself following birth, even if its heart was still beating. On the rare occasions where a child's birth was registered in such circumstances and died shortly after, both the birth and death registrations were subsequently cancelled in the registers, under the authority of the sheriff.

Adoption

Adopting a child in Scotland was not placed on a legal footing until the passage of the Adoption of Children (Scotland) Act 1930. Before this, private adoptions were arranged by charities such as Barnardos (**www. barnardos.org.uk**) and Quarriers (**www.quarriers.org.uk**), which today run research services for those wishing to pursue historic records. Not all adoptions have been made by complete strangers, with step-parents and grandparents among those who have successfully adopted. Informal adoptions may be identified by additions to pre-1930 birth records, or even on census records.

The NRS Register of Adoptions, established in 1930, can only be consulted at the ScotlandsPeople Centre. This provides the date of adoption and the names of the adoptive parents, but no information on the original biological parents. In some cases though, if you have a suspicion as to who the likely birth parents may have been, you might still be able to identify evidence from ScotlandsPeople to help confirm the case.

In one case, I was advised by a client that his mother had been adopted in 1933. She had always known her exact birth date in 1929, but not who her birth mother was. For various reasons, however, he had a very strong suspicion that the adoption might have been made within the family. The person who adopted my client's mother, called Bridget, died in 1980. From her death record, I identified the names of her own parents, when they had married, and the names of their other children; among these I found a much younger daughter called Sarah, who as a teenager had given birth to an illegitimate daughter. The first name of her child was the same as my client's mother's name, and her date of birth also matched exactly. Just for good measure, within the left-hand margin of her birth entry in 1929 was noted the word 'adopted'.

The 1930 Act established that once a child reached the age of 17 he or she could gain access to their original birth record by accessing the relevant court processes surrounding their case; this was changed to 16 by the Children (Scotland) Act 1995. Adoptions were usually arranged by charitable bodies through the sheriff courts (p.132), or occasionally the Court of Session (p.137) in Edinburgh. Once granted, the records were, and still are, individually sealed for 100 years; not even the staff at the NRS are allowed to see them. To ask to view the records, contact the NRS Adoption Unit, based at General Register House in Edinburgh (see **https://**

nrscotland.gov.uk/registration/adoption).
The most recent adoption records may still
be held at the court in question, but older
records will be held by the NRS and you will
be advised on how best to seek access.

There are several agencies that can help
with counselling and support. The Adoption
Contact Register for Scotland is kept by
the Birthlink charity (**www.birthlink.org.
uk**). Other bodies that can help include
Scottish Adoption (**www.scottishadoption.
org**) and Adoption Search Reunion (**www.
adoptionsearchreunion.org.uk**).

In 1869 a scheme was devised for the
Home Office in London to send orphaned
and destitute children overseas to Australia,
Canada, New Zealand and South Africa,
who became known as 'Home Children'.
Placements continued up to 1970. It was
later revealed that some of those who had
been relocated had been exploited in their
new homes, and in some cases physically

*Prior to 1930, adoption
in Scotland was handled
informally by charities and
within families.*

abused. Worse still, many children and parents had been lied to about
their respective fates, with some parents believing that their children
had died, and vice versa, when that was not the case.

The Child Migrant Trust (**www.childmigrantstrust.com**) exposed
much of what happened and now actively seeks to reunite families that
were affected. Library and Archives Canada (**www.bac-lac.gc.ca**) has a
useful 'Home Children – Immigration Records (1860–1939)' database in
its online research section, which includes many Scots children, while
the National Archives of Australia has a comprehensive fact sheet on
child migration at **www.naa.gov.au/collection/fact-sheets/fs124.aspx**

Vaccination

The Vaccination Act of 1863 required all Scottish-based parents to
vaccinate their babies against smallpox from 1 January 1864 onwards,
following the registration of their births, and to have that vaccination
registered. This continued until 1948 when compulsory vaccination was
discontinued.

The 1863 Act allowed for each registration district to be designated
as a vaccination district, within which a suitable medical practitioner

was appointed to administer injections. Each child had to be inoculated against smallpox within a period of six months following birth, and the event to be subsequently registered by the father, mother or primary carer of the child in question. Once the child's birth was registered, the parents or carer were then handed a Notice of the Requirement of Vaccination, which contained several possible schedules, to be filled out and returned depending on how the vaccination appointment went.

The child's name and birth entry details were first recorded into Schedule D of the vaccination notice. The child was then to be taken to the registered medical practitioner within the next six months, who would assess the child and make a determination as to whether it could be vaccinated. If possible, the procedure was carried out, and the Schedule A vaccination certificate was then filled out to confirm that it had been successful. This had to be returned to the local registrar within three days and a record entered into the locally-held birth register, within the left margin.

If the child was deemed temporarily unfit for vaccination but likely to be healthy enough in due course for the process, a postponement could be requested. In such a case, a Schedule B vaccination form was filled out and returned to the registrar, at which point an entry was made into a separate Register of Postponed Vaccinations. Postponement was valid for two months only. The registrar would then immediately fill out another Schedule D vaccination form for the parents to take back to the doctor to try again. This delay could be implemented on several occasions before vaccination finally happened, after which the Schedule A form was finally filled out by the doctor and returned as normal.

If the child was considered by the doctor to be insusceptible to the vaccine disease, a Schedule C vaccination form was filled out and returned to the registrar, who would again record the information into the birth register.

Not everybody was happy with the idea of vaccination, and some refused to have their children go through the process. A few believed that having to submit themselves to vaccination implied that they were from the poorest in society, often the worst-hit by smallpox epidemics. Others were worried about the effects of the procedure, while a few were conscientious objectors, for which there was no legal defence in Scotland until 1907.

Lists of defaulters were regularly handed by the local registrars to parish councils (p.88), usually twice a year, but in larger areas such as Glasgow on a monthly basis. Once received, it was up to the parish council to contact the medical practitioner within the district with an order to vaccinate the defaulters between ten and twenty days after the instruction was issued, the parents having also been notified. The fine for non-vaccination was up to twenty shillings or ten days' imprisonment, but such a sanction was usually applied only with regard to a failure to vaccinate a first child.

Locating Vaccination Records

Vaccinations were recorded within the locally-held birth registers, with the word 'vaccinated' or 'insusceptible' noted in the margins. For this reason the locally-held volumes can sometimes be referred to as the 'vaccination birth registers'. Not all such registers have survived in local registration offices, and where they do exist, you may find additional considerations such as a 100-year privacy rule if the record of vaccination is deemed medically sensitive. A small number of these entries are included in the ScotlandsPeople births database.

The NRS has several interesting holdings concerning vaccination, including court papers for those prosecuted for refusing to vaccinate their children, and correspondence for cases of defaulters (located within the GRO 5 collection). Other interesting collections include a list of 'Statutory Declarations of Conscientious Objection signed by Mothers, Guardians etc of Legitimate Children, from 1914–1916' (GRO 5/351). The kirk session records for Speymouth in Morayshire also include more than 200 vaccination certificates from 1864 to 1878 (CH2/839/54).

Registers of Postponed Vaccinations can be found in several places, but again, closure periods may be in place. The ScotlandsPeople Centre has some registers for Banffshire among its Miscellaneous Manuscript Records collections, for Fordyce (1864–1887, 1885–1947), and Portsoy (1873–1896, 1885–1946). Additional registers may be located in local archives; for example, some in Aberdeenshire and Angus are listed on the SCAN catalogue. The records of parish councils can hold lists of vaccination defaulters, with many surviving in local archives; a good example being those for Kettins Parish Council located at Perth and Kinross Archives. Local newspapers will also carry stories about those prosecuted for refusing to vaccinate their children, and even professionals refusing to perform such vaccinations.

Marriage

The key legal principle which historically underlines the rite of marriage in Scotland is that of consent. Parental permission was not required to marry, nor was a celebrant required to solemnize proceedings prior to 1940.

There were some restrictions on those who could marry. Prior to 1929 it was legal for boys as young as 14 and girls as young as 12 to marry, but this changed to 16 in 1929. There were also several restrictions on who could marry in terms of being closely related through the rules of consanguinity, dating back to the Old Testament book of Leviticus, Chapter 18, and formally embodied in Scots Law as far back as 1567. This stipulated that it was illegal to marry the following:

- An ancestor, descendant or sibling
- Aunts/uncles or nephews/nieces
- An adoptive parent or child
- A wife's sister (until 1907) or a brother's widow (until 1921).

Marriage between first cousins was permissible.

From 1855, the advance proclamation of banns by the Church of Scotland was required prior to a regular wedding taking place. From 1856, a Scottish residency criterion of three weeks was also introduced.

From 1 January 1879, the Marriage Notice (Scotland) Act established an alternative to the calling of the banns prior to a wedding through the use of a marriage notice. For this, the participants had to fill out a form providing the following details:

- Name and surname
- Condition (bachelor, spinster, widower or widow)
- Rank or profession
- Age
- Dwelling place
- Parish (or District) and County in which parties respectively dwell
- Their signature to the appended declaration stating that they knew of no lawful objection to the forthcoming wedding, and date.

Once completed, they would hand it in to the registrar in the district where they had resided within the previous fifteen days, along with a fee of one shilling and sixpence. If both parties lived in the same registration district or parish, a single notice would suffice (filled in on a slightly different form, but with the same required details). The relevant registrar would then fill the details into a Marriage Notice Book, and would also place a public notice of the forthcoming marriage on the door or outer wall of his office. Should anyone wish to consult the Marriage Notice Book prior to the wedding, they could do so upon payment of a shilling for the privilege.

After displaying the notice publicly for seven days, and with no objections received, the registrar would issue the participant or participants a certificate of publication, which was valid for three months. If an objection was lodged, the certificate's issue was withheld until any issues were resolved.

Registration of Regular Marriages

Once the certificates of publication were received, or certificates of the proclamation of banns (or in some cases both: one party could have the banns called, and another go down the notice route), these were conveyed to the registrar at the district where the marriage was to take place. A Marriage Schedule was then issued, without which a marriage could not be carried out regularly. This was handed to the officiating minister at the wedding, and required the following information:

- The date
- The place where celebrated
- The authorization; after banns, after publication, or after both
- The church denomination
- The minister's name
- The contracting parties' details: names, condition, age and occupation, parentage and residence
- Signatures of the contracting parties, the minister and the witnesses.

Within three days of the marriage ceremony the completed form had to be returned to the registrar, upon penalty of a fine up to £10, and the details copied into the Marriage Register. The registrar had to copy the details of the parties' signatures into the register, and not their full names. On ScotlandsPeople, the signatures shown are those written by the registrar, and not the original signatures of the marrying couple or witnesses.

In 1939 the law was changed to permit a Sheriff's Licence as an alternative, in certain circumstances, to the calling of banns or marriage notices. The calling of banns was finally abolished by the Marriage (Scotland) Act 1977, as were marriages performed with a Sheriff's Licence, and the twenty-one-day residency requirement. From 1 January 1978, marriage notices became the sole requirement for advance publication.

Irregular and Civil Marriages

Until 2006, Scots Law distinguished between what were known as 'regular' marriages and 'irregular' marriages. From early in the thirteenth century marriages were deemed regular if the banns were called in the local Church of Scotland parish kirk on three successive Sundays prior to the wedding happening, and the ceremony performed by the church minister.

Irregular marriages, on the other hand, were marriages not performed by the state church. There were several forms of such marriages still valid from the advent of civil registration:

Marriage by declaration: Also known as 'declaration de praesenti', this involved a declaration of marriage in the presence of witnesses (usually two), with no minister or celebrant required to oversee proceedings. It was abolished from 1940.

Betrothal followed by intercourse: Also known as 'promise subsequente copula', this was based on a promise of marriage followed by consummation. It was abolished from 1940.

Marriage by habit and repute: A man and woman living together as if married, and considered to be so by those around them. It was abolished from 2006.

Marriage by declaration was by far the most common form. A nineteenth-century song entitled *The Tourist's Matrimonial Guide Through Scotland* notes the ease by which it created a union:

> The maxim itself might content ye
> The marriage is made by consent
> Provided it's done *de præsenti*
> And marriage is really what's meant.
> Suppose that young Jocky or Jenny,
> Say 'We two are husband and wife.'
> The witnesses needn't be many,
> They're instantly buckled for life.

(Neaves, Lord Charles (1879), *Songs and Verses, Social and Scientific*, Edinburgh; Blackwood, pp.99–102. **https://archive.org/details/ songsandversesso00neavuoft** accessed 9 April 2019.)

Not everyone registered their irregular marriages with the state from 1855, despite it being a requirement, but with the development of the welfare system, it became increasingly advantageous to do so. If a couple wished to register their marriage by declaration, they first needed to record it in writing, merely noting their acceptance of each other as spouses, and to then have two witnesses sign the document also. Within three months of this being done the couple could petition the local sheriff for permission to register the event. A petition warrant was filled out by the couple, and also signed by the witnesses. All four would then appear before the sheriff and swear on oath that the document was accurate and that a marriage had been agreed. As long as one of the couple at least had satisfied the required residency criteria, the sheriff would then issue a warrant for a registrar in the relevant district to record the marriage within the relevant register. A fee of five shillings had to be paid to the registrar in order to obtain an extract of the entry.

It was also possible to obtain proof of an irregular marriage by conviction from a competent court or by a justice of the peace or magistrate, based on laws passed in the seventeenth century (p.46). An amendment was made in the law via the Marriage (Scotland) Act 1916, to stop people going for the option of conviction before a justice of the peace, which was all too often abused as a process as it was much cheaper.

By the 1930s, some 90 per cent of marriages were performed regularly via religious ceremonies, but there was growing agitation for changes within Scots Law to address the forms of irregular marriage, of which there were some 4,000 a year. Between 1926 and 1935 there were 2,295 marriages performed at the blacksmith's shop at Gretna Green alone, of which only 419 were registered with the state. A committee was set up in 1935 by Sir Godfrey Collins, the Secretary of State for Scotland, to look into possible reform, and as a consequence of its findings, the Marriage (Scotland) Bill was introduced to the House of Commons in 1939. This recommended the abolition of marriage by declaration and marriage by betrothal and intercourse, to be replaced with a form of marriage to be performed by civil registrars. The exception, however, was marriage by habit and repute, which was to be retained in statute for those for whom documented evidence of marriage could not be easily secured. This was eventually removed from Scottish statute via section 3 of the Family Law (Scotland) Act 2006.

The provisions of the subsequent Marriage (Scotland) Act 1939 became effective from 1 July 1940. It allowed for the implementation of a civil form of marriage in Scotland, to be performed by registrars as celebrants, as had been the case in England and Wales for well over a century beforehand. Registrars could now perform civil ceremonies within register offices.

The Civil Partnership Act 2004 introduced the concept of civil partnerships into law from 5 December 2005. A civil partnership ceremony is secular and must not contain any religious content, or be held at any place that is 'used solely or mainly for religious purposes'. A prior notice must be given to a registrar within three months preceding the event, and no later than fifteen days before the ceremony is due to happen. The minimum age for both contracting parties is 16, and the usual rules of consanguinity, marital status, etc., apply. The Marriage and Civil Partnership (Scotland) Act 2014 further provided for the marriage of persons of the same sex.

Locating Marriage Records

Marriage records from 1855 onwards have been digitized and placed on the ScotlandsPeople database. The online version imposes a seventy-five-year closure period for images, although indexes are available for more recent events. Images for more recent records can be viewed at the ScotlandsPeople Centre and its equivalents across Scotland. FamilySearch also provides indexes for marriages from 1855 to 1875 within both the IGI and its Scotland Marriages 1561–1910 collection. These note the names of both spouses, and the date and place where the marriage was registered.

The details for a marriage were initially recorded in the Registry Books according to the forms of the Schedule C appended to the 1854 Registration Act, subsequently amended. From 1856 each entry contains the following details:

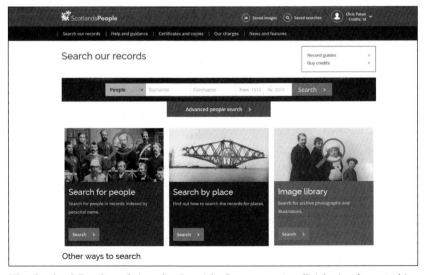

The ScotlandsPeople website, the Scottish Government's official site for searching government records and archives.

- The date and location of the marriage
- Whether an irregular or religious ceremony, and if religious, by which church denomination
- The groom's name, signature, occupation, status (bachelor or widower), age and residence
- The bride's name, signature, occupation (spinster or widow), age and residence
- The parents' details for both contracting parties, including their status (whether deceased), the mothers' maiden names (and additional married names if remarried), and the fathers' occupations
- The name of the officiating minister, or whether by authority of a warrant
- The witnesses' names (and for later entries their addresses)
- The date and place of registration.

In addition, for the year 1855 only, the records contained the following further details:

- The birthplace of each partner
- The number of previous marriages for each partner
- The number of children produced from those marriages.

The birthplace of an individual was eventually restored to the certificates from 1972 onwards. If the bride or groom could not write, an 'X' was recorded instead, with the signature of the registrar noted beside it for verification. If your ancestor was Roman Catholic, you may also find a record of the marriage in the ScotlandsPeople's CPRs (p.32), which includes entries after 1855.

As with birth records, the parental information supplied can be particularly useful in unlocking further family branches and events. In the marriage record for my three-times great-grandparents William Hay Paton and Janet Roger, for example, which took place at Kinclaven on 2 December 1859, William's mother was noted as 'Johan Paton, formerly Thomson, now Fenwick, maiden name Woodroff', identifying three separate marriages for her.

The Register of Civil Partnerships is available for consultation at the ScotlandsPeople Centre, while same-sex marriages are recorded within the marriage register.

Minor Records of Marriage

As with births, there are several Minor Records series concerning the marriages of Scots overseas, which can be consulted on the ScotlandsPeople databases.

The records include marriages located within Army Service Returns concerning Scottish military personnel stationed overseas (from 1885), the Foreign Register (1861–1966), Consular Returns (1917–74) and the Consular and Foreign Records Combined Series (from 1975).

For a detailed listing of the various collections, consult the NRS Minor Records of Births, Deaths and Marriages Overseas guide (p.16).

Divorce

The process of divorce has been possible in Scotland since the sixteenth century, and will be discussed further in Chapter 8. Divorce was handled by the civil-based Court of Session (p.137) from 1830, with the relevant legislation reformed in 1861 and 1938, but the biggest change occurred in 1976 when the Divorce (Scotland) Act allowed for divorce by mutual consent. In 1984, the country's sheriff courts were given the responsibility of hearing cases, a situation which continues to this day.

From 1984 a Register of Divorces can be consulted at the ScotlandsPeople Centre and its equivalents across Scotland. Although images were previously accessible to view, the register is now closed for privacy reasons concerning dependants, with only the indexes available. A useful guide to divorce records can be found on the NRS website at **www.nrscotland.gov.uk/research/guides/divorce-records**

A Register of Dissolutions of Civil Partnership from 5 December 2005 can also be consulted at the ScotlandsPeople Centre.

Registration of Deaths

The need for information on the causes of deaths in the country, the ages at which people died and the frequency of deaths in communities were just some of the key factors that finally convinced the state in Scotland to implement the civil registration system from 1855.

The Registration Act of 1854 required that following the death of an individual, the nearest relative to the deceased, along with the occupier of the house or tenement in which the death took place, should within eight days following the death report it to the registrar, unless the occupier was the deceased, in which case an inmate of the house was to assume the role. Failure to do so could lead to a fine of twenty shillings. In certain cases, the informant may have been a neighbour if no-one more immediately connected was available. Deaths were to be recorded in the parish or registration district where the event happened and not in the home parish of the deceased. In cases where death was not in the parish of residence, then the 'usual residence' was recorded in the register alongside the details of where death occurred.

If death was not registered by those who were required to do so, then such persons (or any other person present at the death) could be formally required in writing by the registrar to attend within fourteen days to provide the required information on the causes of death, upon pain of a forty shillings fine. The need to do so was rare, however, with most people registering deaths within three days by the turn of the century, mainly because a death certificate was required to claim on life assurance policies.

If a death occurred away from a house or a tenement, the occupant of the house was required within twenty-four hours of becoming aware of the event to inform the local registrar, again on penalty of a forty shillings fine. If the residence of the deceased was not known, however, the registrar was to immediately inform the procurator fiscal (p.134) of the event, who would make enquiries. The fiscal was also called in where it was apparent that death had occurred by violent means, or when no apparent cause of death was obvious, even if the deceased's residence was known. If an investigation was undertaken by the fiscal, its conclusion was to be reported to the registrar of the parish or district where the death occurred and entered into the register, either by the fiscal acting as the informant or by the original informant registering the result, and the fiscal's conclusions then being noted within the RCE (p.31).

From 1855 to 1860 only, Scottish death records helpfully list the burial ground where the deceased was laid to rest and the undertaker responsible.

In addition to the informant, a doctor was also required to provide a Medical Certificate (a Schedule G form as appended to the Registration Act of 1854), to the registrar outlining the causes of death and the duration suffered. Originally doctors had fourteen days to transmit the record to the registrar, but unlike in England and Wales, they could be penalized if they failed to do so, in the sum of £2, which infuriated many. The requirements on doctors were soon after relaxed by an amending act in 1860, with doctors now only liable to prosecution if they failed to send a Medical Certificate after being requested to do so by a registrar. At the same time, the period in which doctors were to do so was reduced from fourteen days to seven. The completed Medical Certificates, once sent to the registrar, remained in his or her custody for a period of five years, after which they could be legally destroyed.

Once the death register entry was completed, the registrar was obliged to give a certified copy of death to the informant (a Schedule I form, as appended to the 1854 Registration Act), to be supplied to the undertaker; he in turn had to forward this to the relevant burial or cremation authorities, with failure to do so incurring a £10 fine.

Locating Death Records

As with births and marriages, historic Scottish death records can be accessed on the online ScotlandsPeople database, with a fifty-year closure period, although indexes are available for more recent events. Images for more recent events can be viewed at the ScotlandsPeople Centre and equivalent centres across Scotland. There are no indexes on FamilySearch for Scottish civil registration death records.

All deaths registered in Scotland from 1855 were recorded according to the form of the Schedule B form appended to the 1854 Registration Act and subsequently amended. They contain the following information:

- The name of the deceased
- Marital status, and name of spouse or spouses (if any)
- The date of death, time, and location (with usual residence also recorded if death was not at home)
- The name of the deceased's father, his occupation, and whether alive or deceased
- The name of the deceased's mother, with her maiden surname, and whether alive or deceased
- The causes of death, length of illness, and the name of the person certifying the death. The causes of death were to include both primary and secondary causes, in the order of their appearance. If smallpox

was the cause, the patient's condition as to vaccination was also to be included: a) no evidence of vaccination; b) vaccination in infancy only, and number of scars; c) vaccinated only after infection by smallpox; or d) vaccinated, but with no scars. If the deceased had been vaccinated more than once, this was also to be noted.

• The informant, and his or her relationship to the deceased.

Again, in the early years there were some further additions. In 1855, the registrar noted the following extra details:

• The place of the deceased's burial and the name of the undertaker who was responsible
• The names of any children born to the deceased, their ages and, if they were deceased before 1855, their date of death.

The biographical details required for the latter were in many cases difficult to obtain, and this requirement was abolished within a year. From 1856 to 1860 the burial information remained in the records, but the names of any spouses from 1856 to 1860 were unfortunately not recorded, although the deceased's marital status was noted.

From 1967, the deceased's date of birth has been helpfully recorded.

A problem that can be found in many cases is inaccurate information from an informant, particularly with regard to the deceased's parentage. If the informant was not a relative there were problems enough, but even relatives occasionally got it wrong. It is not uncommon, for example, to find that a son or daughter has offered the names of the wrong grandparents as parents for the deceased, or has given a wrong age for the deceased at the time of death. If a registrar was dubious about the quality of the information offered, further enquiries could be made for more accurate information.

Some of the illnesses described in early death records can seem incredibly unfamiliar. Tuberculosis, a major problem in nineteenth- and early twentieth-century Britain was previously known by many names, including 'phthisis pulmonala', 'consumption' and 'decline'. Websites such as **www.medicinenet.com** and **http://rmhh.co.uk/medical.html** can help to explain some of the ailments that you may encounter.

Minor Records of Death
As with births and marriages, the NRS also holds many records of deaths from overseas within its 'Minor Records' series, many of which are also accessible via its ScotlandsPeople databases.

In some cases, these 'minor' records are anything but. The most notable collections within the series are the three War Registers. They list the following:

- The deaths of Scots who served in the South African War (1899–1902)
- Those who died in the First World War (1914–19) while serving as warrant officers, NCOs or privates in the army, or as petty officers or ratings in the Royal Navy
- The deaths of those who died from all the armed services during the Second World War (1939–45), though this database is incomplete.

Other collections within the Minor Records for Deaths include Marine Registers (from 1855), Air Register (1949–74), Army Service Returns (1883–1974), and the various foreign, consular and high commissioners' returns. A full listing is again available in the NRS Minor Records of Births, Deaths and Marriages Overseas guide (p.16).

Register of Corrected Entries

A unique aspect of the Scottish system not found elsewhere in the British Isles was the establishment of the Register of Corrected Entries (RCE) for births, marriages and deaths. This was kept in parallel by the locally-based registrars, as well as in Edinburgh at the GROS, and designed to record any changes that were authorized to be made to entries in the original volumes, such authority coming from court decisions, by various provisions made within the registration acts, or by the Registrar General. Corrections made into the local registers had to be immediately forwarded also to the Edinburgh-based equivalent. From 1966 it has been known as the Registers of Corrections, Etc.

There are various reasons why a correction may have been necessary: a happy father, too far gone with drink after the birth of a child, giving the wrong name for his child to the registrar; the result of a challenge to the courts over an illegitimate child's paternity; and the result of an investigation of a procurator fiscal into a suspicious death being some of the more common.

The RCE entries have all been digitized and can be accessed on the ScotlandsPeople database. The online records respect the same closure periods to access for birth, marriage and death records, but it should be noted that whether online or at the ScotlandsPeople Centre, the corrections cannot be searched independently; they can only be searched for if records note that there is an RCE entry in the left margin relating to the original entry.

Chapter 3

CHURCH OF SCOTLAND RECORDS

Prior to 1855 and the advent of civil registration, the most important records for genealogists are those created by churches. The largest and most important denomination was the state church, the Church of Scotland, known more colloquially as 'the Kirk', but records from smaller denominations can be equally useful. Surviving pre-1855 baptism, marriage and burial records for the Kirk are available on ScotlandsPeople, where they are referred to as the Old Parish Registers (OPRs). These are accompanied by registers from many dissenting denominations, as well as records from the Scottish Roman Catholic Church, known as the Catholic Parish Registers (CPRs). Many records, excluding Scottish Catholic registers, are also indexed on FamilySearch.

Church records can be detailed or blunt, but where they do strike gold is in covering most of society, from the humblest agricultural labourer to the monarch. They consist of baptismal, marriage and burial registers, the records of the kirk sessions, the presbyteries, the synods, the annual General Assembly, the deliberations of the parish heritors (landowners and patrons) and considerably more.

Background

At the Reformation of 1560, the Church of Scotland was transformed from the Roman Catholic denomination into a body with a new democratic, Presbyterian form of governance. In its earliest form, the congregation of each parish chose its own minister and elders rather than having one imposed upon it by an unelected bishop or archbishop. The landowners on whose land the churches were built, known as 'heritors', were required to pay a stipend to the ministers accepting a 'calling' on

A statue in Stirling of the firebrand preacher John Knox, who led Scotland through the Reformation of 1560.

their patch, as well as to provide for their accommodation and the upkeep of church property.

Throughout the Kirk's first 130 years of existence, the Scottish Crown tried to exert an influence but was largely kept in check by reformers such as Andrew Melville. When James VI took the throne of England in 1603, however, he vigorously attempted to bring the Kirk of his homeland into line with the Anglican practices of his new southern kingdom, soon imposing bishops to oversee the Kirk's synods and presbyteries, and further Anglican rites through the 'Five Articles of Perth'. When his son Charles I revealed further proposals in 1636 and 1637 to introduce a new Anglican prayer book and mass to Scotland, thousands of infuriated Scots retaliated by signing the National Covenant in protest. The king labelled them as traitors, and threatened to march an army to Scotland to subdue them; the Kirk responded by abolishing his bishops. War was declared by the monarch against these so-called 'Covenanters', which soon fed into a full-scale civil war across the island of Britain, with Charles ultimately losing his head to a short-lived English republic.

Following the Restoration, Charles II reintroduced Episcopacy into Scotland though the Recissory Act of 1661. Some 300 objecting Presbyterian ministers were forcibly removed from their churches and took to preaching in secret open-air meetings called 'conventicles'. When a Scottish archbishop was assassinated in 1679, open warfare existed between the king's troops and the Covenanters during the so-called 'Killing Times'. Charles II then gave way to his brother, James VII, in 1685, alarming both Scottish and English Protestants, with James determined to promote tolerance of all religions, including his own Roman Catholic faith. At the 'Glorious Revolution' in 1688, James was forced to flee from Britain, his place usurped by his nephew and son-in-law William of Orange and his daughter Mary, prompting the Jacobite campaigns of the next half-century. Following this revolution, Presbyterianism was finally cemented as the official form of worship in Scotland.

Despite the new revolutionary settlement, many congregations refused to participate and reconstituted themselves as the Scottish Episcopal Church, gaining strong support in the Highlands and in the east of Scotland. A minor Presbyterian faction styling itself as the 'Cameronian' Church (having followed the teachings of Covenanter Richard Cameron) also broke away, renaming itself in 1743 as the Reformed Presbyterian Church, while in the Highlands, small pockets of Roman Catholicism also survived.

Following the union with England and Wales in 1707, Scottish heritors demanded more influence over appointments to kirk sessions and ministries. This was soon formalized through the UK government's 1712 Patronage Act, prompting internal divisions within the Kirk and leading to various schisms by those objecting to the law and the Kirk's compliance. The Associate Presbytery, formed by Ebenezer Erskine in 1733, was forcibly ejected from the church in 1740 and renamed itself the Associate Synod (the 'Original Secession'), while in 1761, Thomas Gillespie's 'Relief Church' broke away for similar reasons. Having left their parent body, these new denominations soon began to quarrel among themselves.

Following the Jacobite campaign of 1745–46, heavily supported by the Scottish Episcopal and Roman Catholic churches, a new 'Burgher Oath' was introduced in 1747, designed to prevent those who had supported the uprising from ever taking high office again. This prompted further divisions within the dissenting factions into those who would and who would not take the oath. Those who swore it became known as the Burghers, and their opponents as the Anti-Burghers. Over separate issues the Burghers split again in 1798 and the Anti-Burghers in 1806, to form new factions known as the Auld Lichts and the New Lichts, with the New Lichts in each camp firmly set on a more theologically liberal course. By the nineteenth century, in order to survive, a series of mergers then happened, with both New Licht factions uniting in 1820 as the United Secession Church, which in turn merged with the Relief Church in 1847 to become the United Presbyterian Church.

By the early nineteenth century the established Kirk, still dominant, was beginning to lose its grip on society, particularly within growing urban populations created by the Industrial Revolution where its archaic parochial structure could not cope. Two powerful wings soon emerged: the Evangelicals, deeply upset with patronage, which desperately wanted to take the church back to core doctrines established at the Reformation;

and the Moderates, happy to maintain the status quo and to appease the State. Patronage remained the thorny issue, and in 1834 the annual General Assembly voted to create a Veto Act to abolish patronage from the Kirk's proceedings. This was rejected by the Court of Session in 1838, a decision further supported by the House of Commons in March 1843.

While many ministers were content to stick with the status quo, the Evangelicals' leader Thomas Chalmers walked out of the General Assembly in disgust, followed by a third of the Kirk's ministers, in an event that came to be known as the Great Disruption. Abandoning the Kirk – and its adherence to patronage – the delegates instead formed the new Free Church of Scotland. It was not until 1874 that the established Kirk itself finally abandoned patronage, but the damage was done.

Old Parish Registers (OPRs)

Registers for baptism and marriage were introduced in the early 1550s, just prior to the Reformation. The earliest surviving entries are those for the Perthshire parish of Errol in 1553; however, the majority of parishes did not keep records until much later, despite further instructions from the Kirk's General Assembly to do so in 1616 and 1636. Many Western Isles parishes did not record such registers until well into the nineteenth century.

There are several issues to be aware of when consulting the OPRs, most notably the spelling, handwriting and language. Take the following example from the parish of Caputh in 1675:

> 27 of July
> Compired James Plafier in the parish of Banathie and his name be proclaimed with Jonat Pincuk in said parish and confirmed marr 23.
>
> (Marriages (OPR) Scotland, Caputh, Perthshire, 337/01. 27 July 1675)

'Plafier' is in fact a variant of the surname 'Playfair', while 'Jonat Pincuk' is a variant of 'Janet Pennycuik'. The place name of 'Banathie' is an early form of 'Bendochy', while 'compired' is a variant of the Scots word 'compeared', meaning to have appeared before a session or court as a witness.

It pays to know the parochial boundary set-up within Scotland, particularly which parish is adjacent to which. Two people marrying from different parishes may in fact have lived just a couple of hundred yards away from each other. An alphabetical list of adjacent parishes is available at **https://tinyurl.com/coterminousparishes**, while parish maps are found online at **www.oldroadsofscotland.com/statisticalaccountsmain.htm** or within a SAFHS-produced publication called *The Parishes, Registers and Registrars of Scotland* (See Bibliography / Further Reading).

Baptisms

Due to the high mortality rate of children, it was desirable to have a child baptised as quickly as possible. In some parishes parishioners were so superstitious regarding the need for an urgent baptism that occasionally a child might be made ill or even die through their parents' urgent zeal, as they ventured out into inclement weather in search of the parish minister. However, not every child was baptised immediately after birth, and it can be unwise to assume that the baptism date in a parish record was close to the date of birth without further evidence to support this.

Until the late 1700s baptism was commonly performed at the church, with private baptisms frowned upon and even fines imposed, the practice having never been sanctioned by the General Assembly. It was not until the nineteenth century that private baptisms became increasingly more popular.

A baptismal record will usually name both parents, including the mother's maiden name, a useful quirk of Scots Law being that a woman never loses this. The following is a typical example from 1840 as recorded in the Fife parish of Wemyss:

The parish church at Tibbermore, Perthshire. Baptismal records for the parish have survived from 1694.

Augt 28
Barbara lawful daughter of Henry Reid Collier in West Wemyss and
Isobel Dryburgh
    September 20

(Baptisms (OPR) Scotland, Wemyss, Fife. 459/00. 20 September 1840)

In this example, 28 August is the date of birth, while 20 September is
the baptismal date. This is not always apparent, and in many cases the
date of birth will not be listed at all. Note also that the child is listed
as the 'lawful daughter' (rather than a 'natural' child, or one 'born in
uncleanness'), establishing that her parents had been regularly married
by the church and that Barbara was legitimate. If you find a case of
illegitimacy, check the kirk session minutes (p.50) for the parish to see if
there was an attempt to investigate its paternity.

Witnesses are occasionally noted. Usually these will be members of
the family, perhaps a brother and sister of the parents, but there may be
a little more to the reasoning behind those chosen for the privilege. In
the north-east of the country, for example, there was a tradition whereby
the sponsors would be chosen to share the baptismal name of a boy
being christened. The following example is from the parish of Brechin
in Angus:

10 Januar 1657
James Wattson husband to Janet Long hade a man child baptized
named William

Witnesses William Watt William Livingston William Mearns.

(Baptisms (OPR) Scotland, Brechin, Angus, 275/00. 10 January
1657)

Naming Patterns
A Scottish naming pattern was commonly used until the late 1800s, and
may help to predict the names of a child's grandparents. The pattern was
as follows:

The eldest son named after the father's father
The second son named after the mother's father
The third son named after the father
The eldest daughter named after the mother's mother
The second daughter named after the father's mother
The third daughter named after the mother.

Take a mythical couple called Peter and Anna, married in 1783 and shown to have had the following children within a single parish:

John	1788
William	1789
Jean	1792
Peter	1794
Isabella	1797
Anna	1803

If we now apply the naming rule, we get the following possibilities:

John	1788	named after the father's father
William	1789	named after the mother's father
Jean	1792	named after the mother's mother
Peter	1794	named after the father
Isabella	1797	named after the father's mother
Anna	1803	named after the mother

With the fourth and sixth children seemingly named after their parents, this appears to follow the pattern but there are things to be cautious of. Note that Peter and Anna married in 1783, but their first child is not shown to have been born until 1788. It may well be that there is a legitimate reason for this; for example, perhaps Peter was a soldier and served overseas for five years? It is also possible, however, that they may have had children in the gap that were simply not recorded. Peter and Anna may simply not have registered an earlier birth, or may have moved to another parish briefly to find work after their marriage, or during subsequent gaps, and had children in other parishes with the records not having survived.

If a child died in infancy, its name could be given to another in later years. Use of the naming pattern could become complicated if a child had grandparents who shared the same Christian name, with the naming order changed to accommodate this. New names may have been introduced to honour someone in the district, such as a newly-arrived minister. There were also some regional variations with the pattern across the country, such as in Bute where the eldest daughter was often named after the paternal grandmother and the second daughter after the maternal grandmother.

In Orkney and Shetland, the old Norse-derived patronymic name system was further in use until the late nineteenth century. Shetland

Family History Society offers a useful example in its online research tips section:

> Laurence Garthson b. abt 1695 had a son Gairth Laurenson b. abt 1715, who had a son Theodore Garthson b. abt 1851 in Yell d. October 1821 in Norwick, Unst, who had a son William Magnus Theodoreson b. 29 April 1798 in Unst.
>
> (Shetland Family History Society. www.shetland-fhs.org.uk/research-tips: accessed 9 April 2019)

FamilySearch's indexes do not take this system into account, meaning that an entry for someone such as Gairth Laurenson, son of Laurence Garthson, would be presented there as 'Gairth Garthson'. A similar patronymic naming system can also be found at play in many Gaelic-speaking areas, with names derived from parents using elements such as the Gaelic word 'mac' (or the genitive 'mhic') for 'son of', and 'nighean' or 'nic' (a contraction of 'nighean mhic') for 'daughter' and 'granddaughter'.

Some records may be simply beyond interpretation. Witness the following example in Ochiltree, Ayrshire, from 1704:

> Something
> George Something lawful son to what-ye-call-him in Mains of Barskimming was baptized April 9th 1704.
>
> (Baptisms (OPR) Scotland. Ochiltree, Ayrshire. 609/01. 9 APR 1704)

History has tragically failed to record what happened to Clan Something.

Foundlings

During your research you may find an ancestor left as a child on somebody's doorstep by a desperate parent unable to look after it. The following is an example of a record for a foundling child discovered in Perth in 1805 and baptized some two years later:

> November One Thousand eight hundred and five years was Born Elizabeth Mill a Foundling and destitute child Parents names unknown vide Session Minutes the thirtieth day of Eighteen Hundred and Seven and baptised the twenty eight day of June One thousand eight hundred and seven by the Reverend James Scott Minister of the Gospel in Perth.
>
> (Baptisms (OPR) Scotland. Perth, Perthshire. 387/14. 28 June 1807)

The subsequent name given to a foundling child may be based on the name of a saint to which the church was dedicated, the name of the minister, the adopted parents, the parish name, or any number of possibilities, and so will almost certainly not in itself provide a clue to the child's true parentage unless specifically identified. Again, the kirk session records may provide further clues.

Stillbirths in Parish Records

Although a stillborn child will not have been baptized, you may come across an entry in the kirk session records testifying to such a birth having occurred, as in the following example from Perth on 22 January 1812. As part of an antenuptial fornication investigation into Janet Rattray, the session clerk noted that she had become pregnant as a consequence, and that

> … at the time of her delivery she was attended by Dr. Henderson and Dr. Lathow and Mistress Brown Midwife, who continued with her the whole time she was in labour til she delivered of a Child which was dead …

> (Church of Scotland kirk session registers. Perth West Church, CH2/586/1/39. National Records of Scotland)

Despite this tragic consequence, Janet was still subsequently rebuked by the session for her 'said sin'.

Missing Baptisms

A birth or baptism may be missing from the OPRs for many reasons, the first being that it might have simply not been recorded. From 1783 to 1794, for example, the Stamp Duties Act was enacted, requiring all baptisms to be taxed at a rate of three pence upon registration, with a similar charge introduced for marriage and burial records. You may be looking for the wrong name in that a child may have been baptized with a more formal version of his or her name than the pet form by which they were more colloquially known in later life. For example, a Jessie may have been christened as Janet, or a Peter as Patrick.

In some extreme cases, church politics may have come into play. In his *National Index of Parish Registers*, Vol. 12, D.J. Steel notes (p.79) the following:

> During the controversy between Evangelicals and Moderates in the 19th Century parents from parishes where there was a

'moderate' minister would go some distance to seek baptism from an Evangelical one. Norman MacLeod (later the founder of Waipu colony in New Zealand), when a schoolmaster in Ullapool doubted whether his minister was in a state of grace and walked fifty miles to Lochcarron to get baptism for his child, only to find his own minister the guest of the minister there.

It is also possible that the child was not baptized within the established church at all but in a dissenter or nonconformist denomination; some dissenting parish ministers kept very poor records, feeling that it was not their responsibility to keep them. Conversely, you may find dissenter or nonconformist baptisms in a Church of Scotland register for the opposite reason: the established church minister may have felt it *was* his responsibility to record all those in his parish. If a minister's name is noted, double-check that he was in fact a minister of the established church if his denomination is not given. (Biographical details of Church of Scotland ministers are available through the multi-volume *Fasti Ecclesiae Scoticanae* available on Ancestry and the Internet Archive.)

A baptism may not have occurred instantly after birth, but many weeks, months or even years later. With the advent of the Industrial Revolution and the sudden expansion of towns in the late eighteenth century, many people were also beginning to give up on the Kirk altogether as urban society developed at an increasingly hectic pace of life. In some parishes it is estimated that only a third of births were ever registered in the first half of the nineteenth century.

When civil registration commenced in 1855, many people wished to retrospectively record an earlier baptism that had previously not been registered. They were able to do so in the Register of Neglected Entries, which recorded such events if they could be proved from other sources to have happened between 1801 and 1854. The following is an example of the birth of a pair of twins in Grange, Banffshire, recorded in the RNE some twenty-three years after the event:

20th September 1832

James Smith, Sheil, had twins by his wife Margaret Gordon, baptised and named James and Elspet Witnesses Elizabeth Keith and John Gordon both in Sheil.

Regd 5 Novr 1855 on evidence of father.

(Baptisms (OPR) Scotland. Grange, Banffshire. 156/00. 20 September 1832)

Such entries are included within the ScotlandsPeople OPR Births and Baptisms database (p.2).

Marriages

A Kirk-based marriage was deemed legal if performed by a minister in a church after banns had been called, usually three times on successive Sundays. Prior to being wed the couple would be examined by the minister and questioned as to their knowledge of religious teachings such as the Lord's Prayer and the Creed. Getting through the minister's examination was one thing; getting through the public's was quite another, with the banns providing an opportunity for someone to object.

The following are the records of banns registered for the wedding of my five-times great-grandparents Peter McEwan and Janet Leitch in Trinity Gask, Perthshire, in 1771:

Sabbath March 24
Received for proclamation money from Peter McCouan in the parish of Madertie and Janet Litch in thy parish two shillings sterling.
Peter McCouan and Janet Litch proclaimed pro 1mo.

Sabbath March 31
Peter McCouan and Janet Litch proclaimed pro 2do.

Sabbath Aprile 7th
Peter McCouan and Janet Litch proclaimed pro 3io.

(Marriages (OPR) Scotland. Trinity Gask, Perthshire. 396/01. 24 March–7 April 1771)

In this record, Peter and Janet were proclaimed three times on successive Sundays, but it is not always the case that you will find a mention of each time the banns were called, with many registers detailing the first time only. Note the use of the Latin abbreviated phrases 'pro 1mo' (*pro primo* for the first time), 'pro 2do' (*pro secundo* for the second time) and 'pro 3io' (*pro tertio* for the third time), which pop up often in marriage and kirk session records. No date is in fact given for the wedding itself, but it likely took place on the following Friday after the last calling of the banns.

If the couple came from different parishes, the banns were called in each of them, and both parish registers should be checked. If neither register notes where the marriage actually took place, it was usually traditional to do so in the bride's home parish. If the event is only recorded in one parish, check the wording of the entry. In some records you may see a person listed as 'of' a particular place or 'of this parish', while in others a person may be described as 'in' a place. 'Of' can imply ownership of a place, 'of this parish' usually means 'from this parish', i.e. a parish of origin, and 'in this parish' or 'in' a place most usually refers to a tenancy or short-term presence in an area (sometimes a person will be further identified as being a 'residenter in this parish'). However, this is not carved in stone and there are exceptions.

The couple hoping to marry usually had to pay a sum in advance to the session known as 'proclamation money' or 'pledge money'. Part of this went to the parish poor, with the rest held on deposit, which could be forfeited if the couple did not go through with the marriage. Sometimes the pledge was made not with money but with a precious item such as a ring. If they 'scorned the Kirk' and failed to go through with the procedure, the item or sum would be given to the charity of the poor. The pledge might also be forfeited if the wedding festivities got out of hand; for example, if the marriage was being celebrated as a 'penny wedding' (p.45). In addition, the couple had to behave themselves prior to the wedding day, or part of the pledge could be deducted.

Always consult both the marriage register and the kirk session minutes (p.55), even if there appears to be nothing out of the ordinary with the marriage record. Take the following event as described in the OPRs of the Aberdeenshire parishes of Inverurie and Oyne:

30th May 1829
George Clerihew in parish of Oyne and Sophia Chalmers in this parish were contracted and after proclamations on two Sabbaths were married by Minister on 13th current.

(Marriages (OPR) Scotland. Inverurie, Aberdeenshire. 204/00. 30 May 1829)

Clerihew and Chalmers
June 13 George Clerihew in this parish & Sophie Chalmers in the Parish of Inverury were married.

(Marriages (OPR) Scotland. Oyne, Aberdeenshire. 230/00. 13 June 1829)

Now look at the following kirk session records for Inverurie, which cast a different light on the event:

31st May 1829
Penalty of George Clerihew and Sophia Chalmers for thrice proclamation on two Sabbaths 1s 4d

28th June 1829
Geo. Clerihew and Sophia Chalmers after suitable exhortations were absolved for antenuptial fornication Penalty 5s

(Church of Scotland kirk session registers. 31 May-28 June 1829. Inverurie, Aberdeenshire. CH2/196/4 p.315. National Records of Scotland)

Rather than proclaim the banns on three successive Sundays, the couple tried to do so over two weekends, including twice on one day. There appears to have been some urgency to the marriage, and it may come as no surprise to know that they had a healthy baby girl born on 2 August 1829.

The calling of the banns and sometimes the wedding itself were recorded in the marriage registers, whereas payments were usually noted in the kirk session minutes or accounts, although occasior ll· you will find payments listed within the OPRs and marriage banr ν thin kirk session minutes (p.55). A record of such a payment, or of the calling of the banns, is not evidence that a marriage was proceeded with, only that it was planned.

One key point to be aware of when it comes to marriage records within the Church of Scotland OPRs is that from 1834 they do not just record the banns of marriages from that denomination. The Marriage (Scotland) Act 1834 allowed dissenting ministers to perform ceremonies within their churches from this point, so long as the banns had been previously called in the established parish church. This means that when searching the OPR records on ScotlandsPeople between 1834 and 1854, the finding of an entry of banns being called for a couple does not necessarily imply their adherence to the Church of Scotland.

For example, take the following entry from Bothwell in Lanarkshire, recorded on 1 August 1847:

John Johnstone & Mary Campbell both of this Parish 3 days.

(Marriages (OPR) Scotland. Bothwell, Lanarkshire. 625/04. 1 August 1847)

What is not apparent from this record is that the couple were in fact both Roman Catholic, something only later made apparent from the subsequent records found for their family.

There may be clues that can help to confirm the denomination within which the marriage subsequently occurred. For example, if the banns entry provides the name of the minister who carried out the marriage, it may be worth double-checking to see if he was indeed the Church of Scotland minister (see p.41), or perhaps a dissenting minister working in the same parish. A check of the relevant kirk session records might also provide additional information.

Following civil registration in 1855, the prior calling of the banns continued to be a form of pre-publication for a church-based marriage until January 1978 (p.22).

Marriage Customs

Weddings attracted many traditions. When Samuel Johnson visited the Hebridean island of Ulva in 1773, he noted in his memoirs an ancient custom carried out on the island prior to the wedding of a virgin. A tribute, known as the 'mercheta mulierum', was paid to the chief of the MacQuarrie clan in the form of a payment of a crown, although previously done so in earlier times with a sheep. Other island-based wedding traditions include the drinking of ale on Orkney from wooden vessels known as 'cogs', still carried out to this day.

In terms of the planning of a wedding, the months of April and November were deemed by some to be 'lucky months', while the month of May was considered by many to be deeply unlucky, and to be avoided like the plague. The day after the old May Day, 14 May, was a definite no-go area, considered to be a disastrous date on which to marry.

The most popular form of wedding was that of the 'penny wedding', a potentially rowdy affair. The Reverend Alexander Johnston, minister of Monquhitter in Aberdeenshire, in a supplement to the parish's Old Statistical Account (p.95), described how such an event occurred.

When a pair were contracted they, for a stipulated consideration, bespoke the wedding dinner at a certain tavern, and then ranged the country in every direction to solicit guests. One, two, and even three hundred would convene on these occasions to make merry at their own expense for two or more days. This scene of feasting, drinking, dancing, wooing, fighting, was always enjoyed with the highest relish, and until obliterated by a similar scene, furnished ample materials for rural mirth and rural scandal.

(*The Statistical Account of Scotland*, Monquhitter, Aberdeen, Appendix, Vol. 21, Edinburgh: William Creech, 1799, p.146)

This was exactly what the Kirk did not want to see. In some register entries you may find that the minister has asked someone else prior to the wedding to act as a guarantor or 'cautioner' (pronounced 'kayshoner'), and for that person to pledge that certain conditions would be adhered to, on the penalty of forfeiting a sum of money. A good example is the following marriage record from 1694, concerning a Patrick Dunsyre and Janet Lumbsdale from Methel Hill in Fife:

> The whilk day was contracted in order to Marriage Patrick Dunsyre to Janet Lumbsdale both in ys paroch... & David Lumbsdale in methel hill became caution yt yr sould not be promiseray dancing at yr wedding married 18 of may.
>
> (Marriages (OPR) Scotland. Wemyss, Fife. 459/00. 18 May 1694)

The record shows that a David Lumbsdale in Methel Hill, likely Janet's father, was asked to stand as cautioner to guarantee that there would not be any 'promiseray dancing at their wedding'. Promissory dancing, also known as 'promiscuous dancing', was something the church viewed as sinful.

Irregular Marriages

As discussed in Chapter 2, there were several additional methods within Scotland by which a couple could be married which did not require a celebrant and which were considered acceptable under the common law.

The state and the Kirk both conspired to deter irregular marriages, with statutes passed in the seventeenth century to force couples to name the celebrants who carried out their marriages and to punish such celebrants through imprisonment and fines. Whenever discovered, those who married irregularly were themselves hauled up in front of their local kirk session, fined and rebuked. The following is an eighteenth-century example from the East Lothian parish of Gladsmuir:

> Gladsmuir April 23rd 1780
> William Stocks and Elizabeth Corser compeared before the session for their irregular marriage and produced a certificate thereof dated at Edinr March 14th 1780 and subscribed by one Charles Johnston. The Minr rebuked them sharply for their irregularities exhorted them to repent and flee to Jesus Christ as the Saviour of Mankind for pardon – declares them married persons and exhorted them to live as such.
>
> (Marriages (OPR) Scotland. Gladsmuir, East Lothian. 708/00. 14 March 1780)

The parish church at Portpatrick, Wigtownshire, was a popular place for Irish visitors, where they could be proclaimed and married irregularly on the same day.

Edinburgh historically saw the highest numbers of irregular marriages, with celebrants profiting from a thriving trade in the inns of the city's Grassmarket and Canongate. Such marriages became increasingly common in the Borders following the creation of Lord Hardwicke's Marriage Act of 1753, which banned them in England and Wales, though not in Scotland, where English Law did not apply. The result was the busy cross-border marriage trade which soon erupted in Scottish border villages such as Gretna, Lamberton, Ladykirk and Coldstream. A parallel trade also took place in Wigtownshire in the late-eighteenth and early-nineteenth centuries, at places such as Portpatrick and Stranraer where day-trippers from Ireland equally sought the immediacy of an irregular marriage under Scots Law.

The increasing frequency of clandestine marriages being performed deeply upset the Kirk, which as well as losing the spiritual argument for the basis of a marriage was also losing significant income from proclamation money. The following note from the session minutes for Pencaitland in East Lothian shows the methods for dealing with the problem there as it increased:

Pencaitland Kirk 14th Augt 1814

The Kirk Session... hereby does ordain That such person or persons, member or members, of this Parish as shall in time coming be married without the regular proclamation of Banns within the Parish church here, shall for the space of four months from the date of such irregular marriage be deprived of church privileges, and subjected to a pecuniary fine, which in no case shall be less than five shillings Sterl & exclusive of other five shillings as the regular proclamation fee. The Kirk Session at the same time reserves to itself the power of augmenting the fine as the circumstances of the parties or the aggravation of the case may seem to require.

(Church of Scotland kirk session registers. 14 August 1814. Pencaitland, East Lothian. CH2/296/7 p.1. National Records of Scotland)

Deaths and Burials

Record-keeping for Scottish burials was particularly poor, with only about a third of parishes having surviving registers. Records from Aberdeen are the earliest known to exist, dating back to 1538.

While some registers, particularly for city parishes, may record the date of death and burial, and even the cause of death, most will solely provide evidence of payments to hire a mortcloth from the local Kirk session, a black velvet cloth that was draped over the coffin or body of the deceased. These usually offer little detail other than a name and a payment, and so it is often difficult to confirm whether you have found the right person or not. There were often different qualities of mortcloth, and the payments varied for their use, with the amount paid often helping to reflect the deceased's social standing relative to others in the parish. Not everybody hired a cloth from the kirk session, however; many trade incorporations and merchant guilds (p.147) had their own, which could be cheaper to hire. The poor were not charged at all, while children under the age of 10 were usually buried without the use of one.

Occasionally the burial records can be a bit more rewarding. The following record from 1840 in Torryburn, Fife goes beyond simply describing the cause of death:

Nov 18

Margaret Ruthven, Low Terry, was buried, died of old age, aged eighty-nine years.

For many years Meg's tongue was a terror to her neighbours.

(Burials (OPR) Scotland. Torryburn, Fife. 458/04. 18 November 1840)

Many people chose not to be buried in the parish where they lived and died, but within the parish of their ancestors.

Finding the Records

As required by the Registration of Birth, Deaths and Marriages (Scotland) Act 1854 (p.10), all existing Church of Scotland parish registers prior to 1820 had to be transmitted to the Registrar General for preservation at the newly-established General Register Office for Scotland. If such material was recorded in a session minutes book, the subsequent clause of the act allowed for copies of the relevant entries to be made and submitted to the GROS instead, and the original register to be kept locally, after the copies had been authenticated by the local sheriff. Records held within Church of Scotland registers from 1820 to 1854 had to be submitted to the custody of the local registrars only; these in turn were required to be deposited in Edinburgh in 1885. At this point the legislation did not stretch as far as the nonconformist churches, which were under no such obligation to comply. In later years, churches that had seceded from the Kirk and later rejoined deposited their records accordingly.

The OPR records prior to 1855, and some for 1855, have been digitized and placed online through ScotlandsPeople on a pay-per-view basis. The digitized records can also be consulted at the ScotlandsPeople Centre in Edinburgh and at equivalent centres across the country (p.3). A comprehensive overview of the records available is offered by the NRS at **www.nrscotland.gov.uk/research/guides/old-parish-registers/list-of-old-parish-registers**

As well as the digitized OPR registers, the ScotlandsPeople Centre has additional records available, which were also handed into the GROS in the past, and subsequently catalogued under the banner heading of 'Miscellaneous Records'. These are listed at **www.nrscotland.gov.uk/research/guides/birth-death-and-marriage-records/miscellaneous-manuscript-records** and include blotter marriage registers (including sworn affidavits, usually signed by a groom, which testify that no impediments to a forthcoming marriage exist), OPR duplicates and scroll copies, private diaries and registers of church ministers, and kirk session fragments. These records might help if you find that an entry that has been digitized in the OPRs is illegible or lacking in detail.

The centre has a vast library holding printed copies of many published and unpublished collections of BMD material. A full list can be consulted at **https://tinyurl.com/printedbmdcollections**. It further holds a substantial collection of death and burial records, a listing of which can be found at **https://tinyurl.com/deathandburial**

Not all Church of Scotland records were handed into the GROS in 1854, and some can instead be found within kirk session registers at the NRS. In addition, duplicate lists of some records which were handed into the GROS also exist within the NRS collections. A list of holdings from pre-1855 can be found at **www.nrscotland.gov.uk/files//research/list-of-oprs/list-of-oprs-appendix1.pdf**. Diane Baptie's book *Parish Registers in the Kirk Session Records of the Church of Scotland* (p.153) provides a similar list, but also includes information on records beyond 1855.

In addition to kirk session registers, there are a few other resources in which irregular marriages may have been recorded; for example, blacksmith accounts from Gretna Green. A full list of what is known to exist has been published by the NRS and placed online at **https://tinyurl.com/irregularmarriages**. The ScotlandsPeople Centre library has copies of some of these in its library as held within its Miscellaneous Records series; a full description is at **https://tinyurl.com/miscmarriages**, along with details on other irregular marriages records accessible within the Historic Search Room of the NRS.

FamilySearch offers access to OPR indexes through its IGI and its Scotland, Births and Baptisms, 1564–1950 and Scotland, Marriages, 1561–1910 databases. Many local studies libraries and family history societies also have OPR records relevant to their areas available on microfilm, such as the Scottish Genealogy Society library in Edinburgh (**www.scotsgenealogy.com**), while Scottish interest groups in overseas family history societies may hold further copies.

There are several publications for headstone inscriptions available from local family history societies in Scotland. The SAFHS website hosts a particularly useful database of more than 3,500 graveyards in Scotland at **www.safhs.org.uk/burialgrounds.php**, identifying which have had their inscriptions transcribed, whether the records are published or unpublished, and how to access them. The Scottish Genealogy Society has an equally large collection of monumental inscriptions, deaths and burials records, including some unpublished collections. A list of these can be consulted online at The Black Book section of its website at **www.scotsgenealogy.com/Downloads/TheBlackBook.aspx**. Holdings at the ScotlandsPeople Centre are listed at **http://tinyurl.com/monumentalinscriptions**

Kirk Session Records
The members of the kirk session, which comprised elected elders and heritors and were overseen by the minister, was responsible for church discipline in the parish, but also handled a variety of other important

functions within the parish, such as the administration of poor relief and education.

Discipline

The session was primarily responsible with the discipline of its flock. As the lowest level of ecclesiastical court in the parish, it adjudicated on all sorts of cases including minor disturbances of the peace such as drunkenness, blasphemy, swearing and failure to observe the Sabbath, issues for which the offender could be fined or publicly humiliated by being made to wear sackcloth and to sit on a penitent's stool in front of the congregation. The cases which dominate the recorded proceedings of most session records, however, are those concerning 'antenuptial fornication', adultery and illegitimacy.

The following is a good example of a case concerning a family in Arbroath in 1789. The baptismal register noted the following:

Dogood

Born	[blank]
Bap	July 9th
Parents	Thomas Dogood, Elizabeth Blair
Name	Andrew, a natural child

(Baptism (OPR) Scotland. Arbroath, Angus. 272/00. 9 July 1789)

The kirk session register for the parish from October 1788 provides the following additional information:

Octr 31st

After prayer Sedrt. Minister & Elders. There appeared before the meeting Elizth. Blair an unmarried woman in this place & confessed that she has gone with child seven months and dilated Thomas Dogood an unmarried man also in this place as the father of the Child who being called compeared & acknowledges himself Guilty. They were both sharply rebuked for their Sin & Scandal & exhorted to Repentance.

(Church of Scotland kirk session registers. 1 October 1788. Arbroath, Angus. CH2/1414 pp.223–4. National Records of Scotland)

With the kirk session record showing Elizabeth as seven months' pregnant, Andrew must have been born in approximately January 1789.

If a case proved to be too difficult to resolve or involved someone from a neighbouring parish, it could be passed further up to the local presbytery or synod to consider (p.57). In exceptional cases, offenders could be forced to take an 'oath of purgation', and even excommunicated. For matters that were more serious or outwith its jurisdiction, the case could be passed on to the civil authorities to consider (see Chapter 8).

The registers of kirk sessions can be a fascinating source for stories and material concerning your ancestor, as well as information on day-to-day affairs. As such, they are best read through in chronological order for any period when your ancestors may have been in a particular parish. The records provide a great deal of information about contemporary life, the moral standards to which the society was to be held, the value of money, and even the occasional humorous anecdote.

One of the key purposes of the records was to keep an account of parish finances. As well as taking payments for marriage pledges and proclamations (p.43), and the hire of a mortcloth (p.48), they also provide records for the administration of poor relief.

Poor Relief

In 1579 the first Scottish Act of Parliament was passed which can be considered the start of the poor relief system in Scotland, albeit with aggressive kindness. Entitled 'For Punischment of Strang and Idle beggars, and Reliefe of the Pure and Impotent', it sought to both outlaw vagrancy and begging, but to also assist those in genuine need. In 1597, the system was enhanced by transferring all responsibility for the poor law to the kirk session of each parish, with a further law in 1600 allowing each session's poor relief duties to be supervised by its superior presbytery. A further act passed in 1617 enabled justices of the peace (see p.148) and parish constables to help tackle the issue of vagrancy, among others. Orphans of poor folk, as well as children who had known no other life but begging, could also now be taken in and educated by well-meaning folk or placed into a craft or trade apprenticeship. A later statute from 1663 led to the creation of 'correction houses' into which any paupers who were unable to find work were committed, although very few were created.

In 1672, kirk sessions were given further responsibility to oversee the administration of poor relief, working in partnership with their heritors. The Kirk's responsibility for the parish poor continued until the Poor Law (Scotland) Act 1845 transferred the function to the state (p.88), although in many areas this was not a strict cut-off date. The following are examples of claims made by a parishioner in Oyne, Aberdeenshire, recorded beyond 1845:

July 29 1844
6 pecks of meat to Ernest Clerihue 5s 4½d

Nov 3 1845
Ernst Clerihue for the ensuing quarter 20s also for balance of last
qtr 11s 6d

May 5 1846
Ernest Clerihue 11s 5d

June 27 1847
Ernest Clerihue 13s 10d

(Church of Scotland kirk session registers. 29 July 1844–June 27
1847. Oyne, Aberdeenshire. CH2/293/6/41. National Records of
Scotland)

The records often state the name of the claimant and payment only, and
you might only find 'Widow Smith' as the description with nothing else
to show if this was your particular ancestor or not. They also describe
money raised by elders for the poor in the church, or on a visit to people
around the parish, but they will rarely name the donors, instead just
providing a running total per area of the parish visited by a particular
elder.

Testificates
The session could be asked also by parishioners intending to move to
a new parish for a document known as a 'testificate' or a 'certificate of
transference'. This would be handed to the minister of the next parish
to illustrate that the person was of good character, who could then be
accepted as a parishioner in his or her new home. The session minutes
may record the text of such a testificate, or simply note when one was
granted or received, which may help you to trace your ancestors'
movements. The following is an example from the parish of Bothwell:

Testificate in favour of John Blair

The tenor follows

Merns Apprill 22: 1731

That John Blair lived in this paroch from his Infancy untill July
last Behaving himself Soberly & Inofencively free of publick
scandal & Church Censure and my be received into any Christian
Congregation where providence shall order his lott for any thing

known is testified at time and place above att appointment of the session & signed by Henry Hunter minr.

(Church of Scotland kirk session registers. 22 April 1731. Bothwell, Lanarkshire. CH2/556/13 p.32. National Records of Scotland)

The Veto Act
In 1834 the General Assembly of the Church of Scotland passed the Veto Act (p.35), abolishing the right of heritors to choose a parish's minister. A consequence of this is that each Kirk session was now required to compile lists of male heads of families, who were given the vote over future appointments. These lists are recorded annually within most session minutes until 1838, at which point a legal challenge was made against the Kirk's Act. As a census substitute they can be extremely useful.

The Old Scottish website (p.6) has indexed the records for the year 1834, for parishes where such lists are known to exist.

Witchcraft
Within the records you may find records testifying to the hysteria of a parish, or the abuse of the session to try to slander others. In the sixteenth and seventeenth centuries accusations of witchcraft are prevalent in many registers. The following is an example from Kirkpatrick-Irongray in 1691:

David Murihead of Drumpark and his wife being called before the Session and examined anent the strife betwixt them and Janet Sinklar submitted themselves to the will of the Session. Janet Sinklar also submitted to the will of the Session for saying that she doubted Drumpark's wife of murder and witchcraft and is appointed to receive public rebuke before the congregation.

(Church of Scotland kirk session registers. 24 September 1691. Kirkpatrick-Irongray, Kirkcudbrightshire. CH2/1343/1 p.11. National Records of Scotland)

Cases of witchcraft were also heard by the Privy Council (p.133), the High Court of Justiciary (p.132), and justices of the peace (p.148). A comprehensive database of all known cases from 1563 to 1736 is available via the University of Edinburgh's Survey of Scottish Witchcraft website at **www.shca.ed.ac.uk/Research/witches**. The 'Sources and Bibliography' section notes the primary sources used in collating the cases outlined within the database.

Survey of Scottish Witchcraft Database

Survey of Scottish Witchcraft
Scottish History, School of History and Classics, The University of Edinburgh, Scotland

Welcome to the Survey of Scottish Witchcraft Database

To begin exploring the nearly 4,000 records of accused witches and documentation of witchcraft belief, click on one of the options listed below. Should you encounter any difficulties we have help pages along the way to guide you through your searches and to help you interpret your results. We have also provided a comprehensive Glossary of terms used in these web pages that also includes other helpful lists and supplemental reference materials. When you click on the glossary link, a new browser window will open so that you can refer to it throughout your time in our web pages.

Accessing the Database

- **Search the database**
  Allows you to create your own search of the database. You can call up information about accused witches by name, place and date. Or you can examine accusations by choosing specific cultural categories and motifs.
- **Show data using interactive graphs**
  Links you to our online interactive graphing capabilities. You can define and create your own graphs looking at witchcraft through time by county, biographical information, and cultural categories and motifs.
- **Show data using interactive map**
  Opens our online interactive mapping capabilities. This feature plots criteria of your choosing onto an interactive map of Scotland. Here, you can see how witchcraft accusations, cultural motifs, and other factors were distributed across Scotland. Or you can break down Scottish witchcraft accusation by decade to see how the content of accusations changed over time.
- **Download the entire database for detailed analysis**
  Gives you free use of all data recorded for the Survey of Scottish Witchcraft Database. This is meant for people with a specialist interest in the history of witchcraft. The database is in Microsoft Access 97 format and the accompanying database documentation is in Microsoft Word. To use the database, you will need to be familiar with database concepts and software. The database does not have a user interface (i.e. forms) and the project cannot provide any user support.

Survey of Scottish Witchcraft
Scottish History , School of History and Classics
The University of Edinburgh
17 Buccleuch Place, Edinburgh, EH8 9LN

Published for the Survey of Scottish Witchcraft
by Computing Services, The University of Edinburgh
Database and application built by the Information Tools Team
Map data provided by the Data Library

The Survey of Scottish Witchcraft website.

Additional resources for witchcraft trials held through the Crown courts are detailed at **www.nrscotland.gov.uk/research/guides/crime-and-criminals#Witchcraft**

Locating Kirk Session Records

Not all kirk session minutes for the Church of Scotland have survived down the years. The minutes for the parish of Inverness, for example, from 20 January 1704 to 15 April 1707, were destroyed in a fire which raged within the clerk's chamber in the church, an event which also saw the destruction of baptismal, marriage and burial records. The vast majority of surviving kirk session books are held at the NRS, where they have been digitized and made available to view in the Historical Search Room, alongside digitized records for presbyteries, synods and the annual General Assembly (p.57).

Digitized access to these collections was further rolled out across many local archives in Scotland to tie in with the 450th anniversary of the Reformation, including those at Aberdeen, Orkney, Stirling, Inverness, Lochaber, Hawick, and at Glasgow City Archives. It is also planned that in due course they will be placed online through the ScotlandsPeople website. The digitized records have not been indexed, but have instead been 'waypointed', with links to the start of each year's coverage within the collection's records, which must then be browsed. In addition, a partial database of some kirk session entries is available on FamilySearch, within its 'Scotland Church Records and Kirk Session Records, 1658–1919' collection.

To locate which records have been catalogued by the NRS, consult the institution's catalogue (p.1). The reference number for all such records have been prefixed with CH2, so you can use this to your advantage by typing in a place name, say Blackford, in the 'Search for' box, and CH2 in the 'Reference' box. In this case we get the following eighteen results:

CH2/500	Records of Blackford/Blackford Old Kirk Session 1697–1947
CH2/500/1	Blackford Kirk Session – Minutes 1697–1737
CH2/500/2	Blackford Kirk Session – Minutes and accounts 1709–1714
CH2/500/3	Blackford Kirk Session – Minutes, distributions, and collections 1738–1773
CH2/500/4	Blackford Kirk Session – Minutes 1768–1877
CH2/500/5	Blackford Kirk Session – Accounts 1773–1823
CH2/500/6	Blackford Kirk Session – Collections and Proclamation money 1863–1892
CH2/500/7	Blackford Kirk Session – Collections, Sunday School collections 1890–1912
CH2/500/8	Blackford Kirk Session – Collections 1893–1910
CH2/500/9	Blackford/Blackford Old Kirk Session – Cash register, special funds 1911–1937
CH2/500/10	Blackford Old Kirk Session – Cash book 1937–1947
CH2/500/11	Blackford Old Kirk Session – Collections for schemes, and Abstract account 1932–1947
CH2/500/12	Blackford Kirk Session – Baptisms 1855–1875
CH2/500/13	Blackford Kirk Session – Proclamations 1855–1861
CH2/500/14	Blackford Kirk Session – Heritors' minutes 1777–1846
CH2/500/15	Blackford/Blackford Old Kirk Session – Stipend and Fiars' prices 1815–1932
CH2/619/41	Presbytery of Auchterarder – Benefice registers of churches in Presbytery of Auchterarder 1971–1975
CH2/620	Records of Ardoch Kirk Session 1834–1977

The first sixteen results are specifically for the kirk session records of Blackford Church of Scotland. The seventeenth result is for the presbytery of Auchterarder, of which Blackford was a member, while the last is for Ardoch, which was created as a chapel of ease in 1781 and converted into a new quoad omnia parish in 1855 by disjoining it from Muthill, Dunblane and Blackford. For other place searches you may get a single result, or perhaps dozens, but all will be connected to your query in some way. Clicking on the blue reference number links will lead you to a detailed description of each holding, while access conditions for each record-holding are noted at the end.

It is important to go through all the results as different record types are not necessarily found catalogued together within the session papers. I once wished to find the kirk session minutes records for West Kilbride, Ayrshire, for the late 1700s and established forty-seven separate catalogue results. The reference numbers CH2/874/1 to CH2/874/6 listed six periods of coverage for the kirk session minutes from 1802 to 1957, followed by various other papers. It was not until CH2/874/40 was found that I came across a further set of kirk session minutes from 1716 to 1802. The reason was simple: this register had been presumed lost when the initial records were deposited, but was subsequently found, handed into the NRS, and duly catalogued much later.

Not all kirk session records have been digitized. So poor was the physical condition of the above-mentioned register for West Kilbride, for example, that I had to obtain special permission to view it under supervision. The book was deemed to be so fragile that it was not possible to digitize it until it had been properly conserved. It is therefore worth checking the access status given for all returned catalogue descriptions. In many cases the original registers have since been returned to archives in the region from where they were first obtained.

Further kirk session minutes are held by the NRS on microfilm, having been contained within the church registers for births and marriages which were handed into the General Register Office for Scotland following the Registration (Scotland) Act of 1854 (p.10). These can be examined at the ScotlandsPeople Centre, with a full listing of such records available listed at **www.nrscotland.gov.uk/files//research/list-of-oprs/list-of-oprs-appendix2.pdf**. Additional records survive in archives around the country, and can be sourced through the SCAN catalogue (p.4).

FamilySearch has microfilms for some registers, which can be accessed in digital form at its family history centres.

Presbytery, Synod and General Assembly
The kirk session was the lowest of the church courts. Each session regularly sent a delegation of ministers and elders through to the local presbytery, which acted both as a court of appeal and as a referring body for more complicated issues on which ministers required guidance. In turn, the presbyteries sent through representatives and cases to their higher provincial synods, of which there were sixteen. These met once or twice a year, but were finally abolished in 1993. To establish to which

presbytery and synod a parish belonged, consult the relevant entry for the parish in the Statistical Accounts of Scotland (p.95).

The General Assembly was, and still is, the highest court within the church. It not only has the power to act as the last court of appeal, it equally had the power to try its own ministers, and to legislate for the good governance of the church and its flock. A book entitled *The Acts of the General Assembly of the Church of Scotland*, listing the main acts passed from 1638 to 1842, can be found on Google Books at **https://tinyurl. com/4crl4fp**, as can some published assembly minutes of the 1830s and 1840s.

The registers of many early General Assemblies were destroyed in a fire in 1834, but the surviving records were deposited with the NRS in 1961. The records held here are catalogued under CH1, while presbytery and synod records are filed under CH2 (as with the kirk session papers).

Heritors

The role of heritors was essentially to finance the church and its minister, the school, the parish poor, and any other activity crucial to the successful running of the parish. Following the Glorious Revolution (p.33), heritors agitated for a greater say in the running of an operation that they were helping to finance. They secured the right of patronage from 1712 until 1874, which allowed them a say in the choice of any new minister, but which proved very unpopular in many parts. The newly-called Reverend Thomas Lawrie, for example, had to be escorted to his charge in Bathgate in 1717 by a party of armed dragoons for his safety, having been selected by the main heritor against the popular will. The issue of patronage did much to destroy the unity of the Kirk over the next century.

Heritors' records mainly consist of accounts, including in some instances information on the distribution of poor relief in the parish, but they can also be useful in identifying the appointments of schoolmasters to a parish. In most cases, however, they usually carry some fairly mundane parish maintenance decisions. To identify the names of heritors, consult the kirk session registers, contemporary gazetteers, and the Statistical Accounts of Scotland (p.95).

Locating the records can be hit and miss. Some are held by the NRS, and are indexed with an HR prefix. For example, the records of the heritors of Barony in Lanarkshire can be found under HR554 for the period from 1705 to 1929, with twenty collections identified, including various sets of minute books and accounts, correspondence, papers regarding teinds (the Scots word for 'tithes') and stipends.

Other heritors' records which may contain genealogically useful material may be found within estate papers (p.111), either at the NRS, in local archives or in private hands. For the holdings of local archives check the SCAN catalogue, while to locate estate papers that may still be in private hands you should consult the NRAS. Bear in mind that large estate owners may have moved elsewhere in Britain and taken their records with them, so you may also need to check the English equivalent, now integrated into the Discovery catalogue of The National Archives at **https://discovery.nationalarchives.gov.uk**

Chapter 4

OTHER CHURCHES

By 1855 there were considerably more Protestant and other church denominations in Scotland than just the Church of Scotland. The Great Disruption of 1843 saw a third of the Kirk walking away from the establishment to form its own more evangelical body, the Free Church of Scotland (p.35). Many other dissenting Presbyterian factions had already since left the fold and were no longer under the control of the state, nor affected by its laws on patronage.

Switching Churches
Never assume that your ancestors stayed with the same churches throughout their lives, for there are many reasons why this may not have been the case. In smaller parishes the Church of Scotland may have been a constant presence in the landscape, but the story within more urbanized environments was considerably different. As the population of cities grew during the Industrial Revolution, many churches were so overcrowded that 'chapels of ease' were erected to help share the burden within the set boundaries of the parish. Many of these bodies were later erected into parishes in their own right.

Whether based in rural or urban Scotland, it was also possible that family members switched to new denominations through religious conviction or by necessity. A good case concerns my Henderson ancestors in Kinclaven, Perthshire. My six-times great-grandparents Andrew Henderson and Jean Bennett had at least six children – Peter, William, James, John, James and Jean – but while I was easily able to identify the baptisms of the last five within the Church of Scotland OPRs, the record for my five-times great-grandfather Peter was strangely absent. It was eventually discovered that Peter had in fact been baptized in 1755 at the Associate Session of Kinclaven, one of the first churches to break away from the Church of Scotland during the first secession led by Ebenezer Erskine (p.34). Peter's baptism, found under the name variant of Patrick, was included on 2 November 1755:

> The Revd Mr Robert Carmichael Minister of the Gospel at Coupar Angus baptized a child to the Revd Mr Alexr Blyth Minister of the Gospel in this Associate Congregation called Kathrine – and another this same day to Andrew Henderson in Kinclaven parish called Patrick.
>
> (Kinclaven Associate Session, Minutes 1747–66, 1770–80, Baptisms 1747–55. Kinclaven, Perthshire. NRS CH3/502/1. 2 November 1755. National Records of Scotland)

Following a ministerial vacancy in the Associate Session after 1755, Andrew and Jean switched back to the state church instead.

Never trust that you have found the full story concerning religious adherence from a first record find alone, with the following an example that illustrates the point well. I was asked to do some research into a family by the name of Bowes (aka Bows), and had discovered that a John Bows and Lillias Paterson had married in 1755, with the banns called both in Eastwood and Cathcart. The Church of Scotland OPR registers recorded the banns as follows:

> Bows & Paterson
> John Bows in the Parish of Cathcart & Lilias Paterson in this parish gave up their Names for Proclamation in order to Marriage this 11th of April 1755.
>
> (Marriages (OPR) Scotland. Eastwood, Renfrewshire. 562/00. 11 April 1755)

> April 12 1755
> Bows & Paterson
> John Bows in this Parish & Lillias Paterson in the parish of Eastwood, gave up their names to be proclaim[e]d in order to Marriage and paid their dues & having been three times proclaimed Married.
>
> (Marriages (OPR) Scotland. Cathcart, Lanarkshire. 560/00. 12 April 1755)

Ordinarily these might be considered sufficient finds. My problem, however, was that I knew that the couple subsequently had several children, none of whom could be found within the Church of Scotland OPR baptismal records for any parish within the country. After some further research I established that there was in fact a separate Associate Session congregation in nearby Glasgow at the same time, which many people attended from surrounding districts. On consulting the records at Glasgow City Archives, I soon found the baptisms of several of their children. Despite having already located the couple's marriage in the Church of Scotland's OPRs, I decided to consult the Associate Session's marriage register, and much to my surprise found the following:

> Jno. Bowes shoemaker in Cathcart and Lillias Patterson Law[fu]l daug[hter] to Ja[me]s Patterson shoemaker in the parish of Eastwood gave up their names to be proclaimed in order for marriage the 10 of Aprill 1755 and being proclaimed were married

> (Greyfriars Associate Session, Baptismal Register and Proclamations, 1729–1779. Glasgow, Lanarkshire. CH3/469/39. 10 April 1755. Glasgow City Archives)

This record states that the couple's names were given up for proclamation on 10 April, a day before the OPR record for Eastwood suggested this to have happened. John is also noted here as a shoemaker in Cathcart, a useful detail missing from the OPRs which allowed me to search for more on the family within the relevant trade incorporation records (p.147). Lillias' father was further noted here as a James Paterson, also a shoemaker; important details missing from the OPR equivalents.

Finding Records of Dissenters

The records of some dissenter birth and marriage events have in fact been recorded by the Church of Scotland, and can be found in the main OPR registers on ScotlandsPeople. Occasionally this is blatantly obvious, as in this example from the Lanarkshire parish of Barony in 1852:

> Barras
> Alexander Smith Barras, cotton spinner, Calton & Sarah Anderson, residing there, Married at Glasgow the 30th day of April 1852 by the Revd Alexander Wilson minister of the Free Church in Bridgeton, Calton Parish, Glasgow.

> (Marriages (OPR) Scotland. Barony, Lanarkshire. 622/00. 30 April 1852)

In other records you may first have to play detective for a bit. In the following example I was asked to locate several children to a couple residing in the parish of Anderston in the 1840s. Their baptismal records were not on ScotlandsPeople, but the couple's wedding had been noted twice in Church of Scotland registers, in both the parish of Barony and in Campbeltown, on the Kintyre peninsula:

> 22 August 1833, Anderston, Barony, Glasgow
> James Kelly, shoemaker and Mary Adams residing in Campbeltown were married by the Rev. James Smith of the Relief Chapel, Campbeltown.

> 22 August 1833 Campbeltown, Argyllshire
> James Kelly, shoemaker of Glasgow and Mary Adams of this parish were married.

The Anderston entry noted that the couple had been married by a Relief Church minister in Campbeltown. I searched for any sign of the same denomination being present in Anderston, and established that Anderston Relief Church had existed at 9 Heddle Place. Its records had survived and were located at Glasgow City Archives, and thankfully included a baptismal register covering the years from 1829 to 1856 (catalogued by the NRS as CH3/591/12). A quick search of this then identified the baptisms of nine children to the couple, the records

The Mitchell Library, home to Glasgow City Archives.

confirming the family address at 42 Clyde Street, exactly matching their address as given in the 1841 and 1851 censuses.

In the urban sprawl of a growing industrial city like Glasgow, it may be difficult to narrow down the possibilities for the church denomination of your ancestors. If there are no clues from the records you have, you may have to dig out a contemporary map and try to identify which churches were in the area where your ancestor resided, and literally work through them one at a time. The National Library of Scotland's online maps and street directories at **www.nls.uk** can be immensely helpful with this. For example, the Glasgow 1851–52 Post Office directory appendix includes more than five pages' worth of listings for the established Church of Scotland (38 churches), Free Church of Scotland (38), United Presbyterian Church (26), Reformed Presbyterians (2), Original Seceders (2), Church Presbyterians (1), Independents (5), Independents not in Connection with the Congregational Union (3), the Evangelical Union (2), Old Independents (1), Baptists (5), Episcopalians (6), Wesleyan Methodists (1), Wesleyan Association (2), Roman Catholics (10), and Unitarians (1).

Another useful way to establish contemporary denominations within a place is to consult a gazetteer or directory, or a published history of the area in question, such as the Statistical Accounts of Scotland (p.95). The following is a brief description from the second account of Kinclaven in Perthshire, as described by the Reverend Henry Henderson in June 1843:

> The number of communicants at the sacrament amounts to 180. There are 86 families, including 413 individuals, belonging to the Established Church, and 96 families, including 465 individuals, who belong to the United Secession. It may also be mentioned that, within these few months, three Roman Catholic families have been brought to the parish, as servants to the Rev. Mr Mackay, the clergyman of the Roman Catholic church in Perth, who has obtained in lease a farm of seventy acres on the Arntully estate, which he is improving at great expense.

> (*The New Statistical Account of Scotland, Kinclaven, Perth*, Vol. 10, Edinburgh: Blackwood and Sons, 1845, p.1137)

If you have a Roman Catholic ancestor from Kinclaven, it not only points to the fact that they lived in Airntully, it also gives the name of the priest and his place of work. For most people with connections to the parish, however, the record shows that the majority were dissenters belonging to the United Secession, i.e. the Associate Session (or 'Original Secession'), established following the split from the Kirk in 1740 (p.34).

Many records from dissenter churches have been deposited with the NRS, and are now available on ScotlandsPeople, in the 'Other Churches' category. Other events have also been indexed by FamilySearch within its IGI and Scottish baptism and marriage databases (p.5); they are easily identifiable as dissenter entries, with the denomination name listed after the parish (for Church of Scotland records, only the parish name is given).

Other registers from across the country have been catalogued by the NRS but retained by local archives. As previously noted, Church of Scotland records have been classified by the archive under the number CH2. The records for the following dissenting Presbyterian denominations are instead classified under CH3:

Associate Synod	from 1733
Relief Church	from 1761
General Associate Synod (Antiburgher)	from 1747
Associate Synod (Burgher)	from 1747
United Association Secession	from 1820
Original Secession Synod	from 1827
Free Church of Scotland	from 1843

The registers of some Free Church of Scotland congregations are also classified under CH13, as are those of the United Free Church (formed by a merger in 1900 between most of the Free Church of Scotland and the United Presbyterian Church, itself formed by a merger between the Original Secession and the Relief Church in 1847). These registers were handed in following the re-unification of the established Church of Scotland with the United Free Church in 1929.

The dissenter records of the NRS are also listed through the SCAN catalogue, along with listings of additional records held in some local archives. One of the more confusing aspects of the dissenting Presbyterian faiths is their constant splits and mergers. Although the same church building may have played host to a congregation for more than a century, its denomination and name may well have changed on a regular basis. In most cases, a potted history of such developments is included within the catalogue descriptions on both SCAN and the NRS.

Diane Baptie's excellent guide book *Registers of the Secession Churches in Scotland* (2000, SAFHS) will be of immense assistance in locating records. It describes the records available for the Reformed Presbyterian Church, the many denominations which came together in 1847 to form the United Presbyterian Church, and the Free Church of Scotland from 1843.

In addition to the NRS, some printed transcripts and photocopies of additional Free Church records are held at the ScotlandsPeople Centre's library, via its Miscellaneous Records series. A listing of these is available at **https://tinyurl.com/freechurchrecords**

Other Church Denominations
Alongside the many Presbyterian denominated churches, several other faiths set up shop within the country, most notably the Scottish Episcopal Church in the 1690s, and the resurgent Roman Catholic Church, particularly after the Irish Famine of the late 1840s.

In addition, many much smaller faiths found their way into the Scottish religious tapestry. For example, Baptists briefly arrived in the early seventeenth century before returning to Glasgow in 1762, while Quakers also established themselves for a short while in the north-east in the mid-seventeenth century, particularly in Aberdeenshire and much later in Edinburgh. Some of these churches have deposited their registers at the NRS, while others may still be held by the original parish churches or in local archives. In addition, the ScotlandsPeople Centre library may also have relevant resources.

For further details on the history of these denominations consult D.J. Steel's *National Index of Parish Registers Volume XII: Sources for Scottish Genealogy and Family History* (1970, Phillimore). Listed below are brief summaries of the most notable, with particular emphasis on the Episcopal and Roman Catholic churches and, where known, the location of relevant records.

Scottish Episcopal Church
In the aftermath of the so-called Glorious Revolution (p.33), the Episcopal wing of the Church of Scotland had been defeated in terms of its ambitions as the state church, with Presbyterianism formally established in its wake. The Episcopal faction's Scottish bishops were invited to give allegiance to William and Mary, but were unable to do so, having previously pledged their loyalty by oath to James VII as their monarch and as head of their church. Their charges were removed, and in due course, as they died, they were replaced by 'College Bishops', bishops in name only without dioceses to administer.

Between 1689 and 1690 more than two-thirds of Scotland's 900 parishes saw their Episcopal minister ejected from the pulpit and a new Presbyterian minister installed in his place, although not always immediately, leading many parishes to endure vacant seats for some time. In some areas the Episcopal minister managed to remain in position,

The Scottish Episcopal Church is today part of the worldwide Anglican community.

while elsewhere, rival ministries were established between Presbyterian and Episcopal ministers, causing virtual chaos. This was particularly a problem in 1695 when a famine hit much of the country, with the different religious bodies arguing over who had the right to collect and administer money for poor relief.

A series of Acts in 1695 allowed many Episcopal ministers to retain control of their parish churches, on the condition that they took an oath of allegiance to the new regime, causing a schism in their membership. While a small number of ministers availed themselves of the opportunity, becoming known as 'jurors', the majority refused and became known as 'non-jurors'. A separate Act forbade these deprived Episcopal ministers from performing baptisms and marriages, the first of many penal laws which allowed the civil authorities and Presbyterian courts to persecute their Episcopal rivals.

In 1707, Presbyterian Scotland and Anglican England united to form Great Britain. As a consequence, the Scottish Episcopalians Act was passed in 1711, permitting Episcopal ministers to organize as an independent body within Scotland, leading to the formation of the modern Scottish Episcopal Church and the right to perform baptisms and marriages. This led to a resurgence of support for the church, not least in Edinburgh where the church's clergy outnumbered their Presbyterian counterparts. The non-juror wing, however, still loyal to James VII and the Stuarts, became strong proponents of the Jacobite cause. Further penal laws were enacted against them in 1715 and 1719, and again in the aftermath of the Forty-Five Rebellion. Most of these laws would not be removed from statute until 1791, following the death of Bonnie Prince Charlie some three years earlier, and the effective end of the Stuart claim on the British throne. By this point, the church had been all but decimated with only forty practising ministers and four bishops left in Scotland.

Throughout the eighteenth century the west and south-west of Scotland were strongly Presbyterian, while central areas such as Perthshire were more mixed in their loyalties between the two factions. The heartlands for the Episcopal faith were predominantly in the north-east of the country, in Aberdeenshire, Kincardineshire, Moray and Angus, and in parts of the Western Isles.

Locating Episcopal Church Records

The records of the Scottish Episcopal Church are to be found in various locations, not least with some still remaining with the original parish that generated them. A dated but still useful list of known surviving records and their locations is included within D.J. Steel's *National Index of Parish Registers*, Vol. XII (*ibid*, pp.244–248). The NRS has a substantial collection of deposited material from much of lowland Scotland, particularly around Edinburgh, catalogued under CH12.

Other records are held in archives across the country. For example, the registers for the city of Aberdeen are held at Aberdeen City and Aberdeenshire Archives (**www.aberdeencity.gov.uk/archives**), but those for St Andrew's Cathedral in Aberdeen and in surrounding historic Aberdeenshire are held at the University of Aberdeen's Special Collections Centre (**www.abdn.ac.uk/special-collections/index.php**) as part of holdings for the Diocese of Aberdeenshire and Orkney. Other Episcopal records for the historic counties of Kincardine, Angus and Perth, as part of the former diocese of Bechin, are held by the University of Dundee's Archive Services (**www.dundee.ac.uk/archives**).

For the rest of the country, consult the SCAN and NRAS catalogues, as well as catalogues for local archives (p.4). Scottish family history societies may have publications with records of interest, while some transcribed Episcopal records from Aberdeen, Midlothian and Fife can also be found within the 'UK Parish Baptism, Marriage and Burial Records' collection on Ancestry.co.uk.

A brief history of the Scottish Episcopal Church by Gerald Stranraer-Mull is available at **https://tinyurl.com/ScottishEpiscopal**

Roman Catholicism

In the immediate aftermath of the Reformation of 1560 (p.32), Roman Catholicism continued in many places, until the abdication in 1567 of the Catholic Mary, Queen of Scots, which was followed by a clampdown on preachers unwilling to conform to the new Protestant regime. A Counter-Reformation commenced in the country in 1581, but by 1593 all Catholic priests were ordered to leave the country upon pain of death. Following James VI's move to London in 1603 and the subsequent attempt on his life a year later at the Houses of Parliament (the 'Gunpowder Plot'), a series of penal laws were enacted against priests caught preaching in the country, with many lairds' estates also confiscated if it was found that they had converted to the religion. Further persecution followed in 1628, and again in 1638 following the signing of the National Covenant. While some nobles worshipped in secret chapels, others attended Episcopalian services and hid their Catholicism, simply taking communion annually. Other lairds were forced to hand over their sons to be raised through the Episcopal regime.

Following the Glorious Revolution in 1688, there was renewed persecution against Catholics, with many now signed up to the Jacobite cause, particularly after the Forty-Five Rebellion. More than 1,000 adherents were killed and banished following a proclamation that all Catholics were now outlaws. Nevertheless, Catholicism continued to survive.

In 1793, the Catholic Relief Act finally freed the faith from much of its persecution in Scotland, a task completed by a further Act of 1829. The religion began to see an increase in the number of followers, particularly from people arriving from Ireland to take up work as the Industrial Revolution took hold towards the end of the eighteenth century. Despite the increase in numbers, it was with the arrival of refugees from the Irish Famine in the late 1840s that the religion was dramatically 'rebooted' to become a mainstream denomination once again, as it remains today.

In addition to the Irish, other notable waves of more recent immigration have included Italian, Lithuanian and Polish Catholics, with many of the latter based in Lanarkshire and worshipping at sites such as the Carfin Grotto near Motherwell (**www.carfingrotto.org**).

Locating the CPRs
Due to the persecution of Catholicism, it was not safe to keep parish registers for much of the three centuries following the Reformation. The majority of surviving Roman Catholic records therefore relate to parishes in existence from the 1840s onwards, after the flood of migrants from Ireland's famine-stricken land dramatically re-invigorated the church's congregations in Scotland.

In addition to the detailed post-1855 civil registration birth records, it is still well worth consulting the Catholic baptismal records as they usually list godparents, often siblings of the baby's parents, which may provide extra clues about your family. Records of the Roman Catholic Church in Scotland are held by the Scottish Catholic Archives (SCA) in Edinburgh (**www.scottishcatholicarchives.org.uk**). A list of the surviving parish registers, and their years of coverage, can be consulted in the Family

History section of the archive's website. Its Historic Collection of pre-1878 records is on long-term loan to the Special Collections Centre of the Sir Duncan Rice Library at the University of Aberdeen (**www.abdn. ac.uk/library/using-libraries/the-sir-duncan-rice-library-123.php**), while records of the Archdiocese of Glasgow (**www.rcag.org.uk**) are held by its own dedicated archive at 196 Clyde Street, Glasgow. Additional records concerning the Roman Catholic Church's business and organization in Scotland are held at the Pontifical Scots College, Rome (**www. scotscollege.org**), and the Royal Scots College in Salamanca, Spain (**https://scots-college-salamanca.org**).

Copies of the SCA's baptismal and marriage registers for 99 parishes are held by the NRS (under RH21), while the records for some 116 parishes have been digitized and made available on FindmyPast, the ScotlandsPeople website and in the ScotlandsPeople Centre, as well as through other archives and registrars' services hosting the database. These Catholic Parish Registers (CPRs) record births and baptisms from 1703 to 1992, banns and marriages from 1736 to 1934 and deaths and burials from 1742 to 1955. A list of parishes and churches, and the available coverage for each, is accessible at **www.scotlandspeople.gov. uk/guides/church-registers**, while a series of parish maps can be found at **https://tinyurl.com/CPRparishmaps**

The ScotlandsPeople hosted records also include registers sourced from the Roman Catholic Bishopric of the Forces (**www.rcbishopricforces. org.uk**) based in Aldershot, England, which is responsible for the chaplaincy of all Catholics within the United Kingdom's military establishments around the world. They include vital record entries dating back to the mid-nineteenth century, with material from bases in Britain, Singapore, Alexandria, Cairo, Malta, Cyprus, Germany, Austria, Lebanon, the Middle East and the Far East.

One other major database addition for these records on ScotlandsPeople is that for 'Other Events', which contains additional treasures. These collections cannot be searched individually, but include a variety of possibilities, such as communicants lists entries, confessions registers entries, confirmation records, seat rents, sick calls (detailing visits by a priest to sick parishioners), and 'status animarum' records, meaning 'state of the souls', essentially a form of church census. Roman Catholic confirmations occurred with children aged between 7 and 12, and in addition to details on the child you may be lucky to find further information on other family members. The confession registers unfortunately do not provide details of the discussion between a parishioner and the priest, merely that a confession was heard!

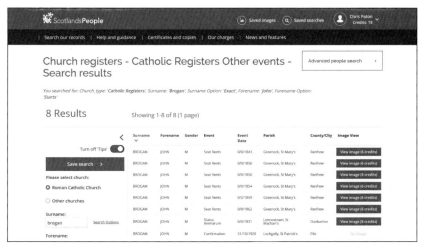

The 'Other Events' category for Roman Catholic records on ScotlandsPeople offers a variety of events, including seat rents, status animarum records and confirmations.

Note that the ScotlandsPeople Centre in Edinburgh also holds a vast amount of additional Catholic-based material, including printed collections of registers, monumental inscriptions and Catholic directories. A list of these can be found at **https://tinyurl.com/SPCentreCatholic**

Finally, a comprehensive genealogical guide to Roman Catholic records in Scotland is Andrew Nicholl's *Scottish Catholic Family History* (2011, Aquhorties Press), while David Dobson's *Scottish Catholics at Home and Abroad 1680–1780* notes occurrences of Scottish Catholics from a variety of additional sources (2010, Clearfield).

Smaller Denominations
There were many other minor denominations in Scotland, which will now be considered.

Society of Friends
Also known as the Quakers, they first became active in Scotland during the Cromwellian period of the 1650s, notably in Dunbartonshire, Lanarkshire, Stirlingshire and Aberdeen. In 1661 a Parliamentary Act sought to persecute followers of the religion in Scotland, but it continued to gain ground in Edinburgh, the Borders, and in particular Aberdeenshire, with Aberdeen becoming home to one of the longest-established meetings. However, in the nineteenth century, adherence to the religion began to decline across the country, despite some minor revivals. Nevertheless, some meetings continue to this day, with further information available at **www.quakerscotland.org**

Many Quaker records and registers from across the country are now deposited at the NRS, catalogued under CH10/1-4. The ScotlandsPeople Centre lists some additional transcribed holdings at **https://tinyurl.com/ NRSQuakerRecords**, while the Society of Friends also has a library in London, with a catalogue available on its website at **www.quaker.org.uk**

Methodists
The Methodist Church first gained traction in Scotland following visits from England by John Wesley and Christopher Hopper in the mid-eighteenth century.

While a Methodist Society was established in Dunbar in 1755, the first Methodist chapel was founded in Aberdeen some nine years later in 1764, to be joined soon after by chapels in Edinburgh, Dunbar, Arbroath, Glasgow, Inverurie, Dumfries and Dalkeith. Preaching rooms and societies were formed across the country, and several 'circuits' established. By Wesley's death in 1789, however, the denomination's progress had been slow, with just 1,179 members across the country. This doubled by the 1820s, but later expansion in the twentieth century was largely due to English settlers in Scotland rather than by native adherents. While Methodism never became a mainstream branch of the church in Scotland, it did contribute towards the evangelical revival in Scotland in the late-eighteenth and early-nineteenth centuries.

As with Presbyterianism, there were many Methodist factions, including the Primitive Methodists, who established several meetings from 1826; the Methodist New Connexion in Glasgow from 1810; three short-lived latter nineteenth-century Independent Methodist chapels in Glasgow (Charlotte Street, Suffolk Street and Low Green Street); the Wesley Methodist Association from 1836; and United Methodist Free Churches from 1857.

If your ancestors were Methodists, the NRS has circuit and chapel records catalogued under CH11, while a ScotlandsPeople Centre guide to its Methodist record-holdings is available online at **https://tinyurl.com/ SPMethodist** (largely comprising a baptism register for Dundee from 1785 to 1898 and several recent synod directories). Methodist records are also held in archives across the country: consult both the SCAN and NRAS catalogues for holdings.

Congregationalists
This was originally a movement set up independently in several parishes across the country in the late 1790s, in which the congregations took full control of their spiritual matters and governance. In particular, it was

promoted by Robert and James Haldane, who set up the Society for the Propagation of the Gospel at Home in 1797; when a Congregational Union was established in the country in 1813, it soon comprised about 100 congregations.

Some records from Congregational churches are held at both the NRS and in local archives, and are catalogued by the NRS under CH14. A handful of holdings are also held by the ScotlandsPeople Centre: see **https://tinyurl.com/scottishcongregational**

Evangelical Union

The Evangelical Union was formed in the aftermath of the Disruption in 1843 by James Morison of Clerk's Lane Secession Church in Kilmarnock, Ayrshire. It soon attracted many from the Congregationalist faith, with the 1851 Religious Census (p.80) showing some twenty-seven congregations in existence by then. In 1897 it merged with the Congregational Union.

A small number of registers are catalogued by the NRS under CH14, while records from other congregations are further listed on the SCAN catalogue.

Baptists

Baptist congregations were first formed in Scotland in the latter half of the eighteenth century, initially in Keiss, Caithness in 1751, and then in Edinburgh in 1768, with the latter congregation and subsequent offshoot branches known as the 'MacLeanists' after founder Archibald MacLean. A split from this denomination in Glasgow led to the English model of the Baptist Church gaining a foothold in Scotland. In the early part of the nineteenth century a Baptist movement spread across the Highlands and Islands, following the work of the Baptist Home Missionary Society established in 1827, and later found a foothold on the east coast within many fishing villages. The various disparate congregations later came together under the Baptist Union of Scotland from 1869, which still exists today (**www.scottishbaptist.com**).

The records of many Scottish-based Baptist congregations are held by the Baptist Union of Scotland at 50 Speirs Wharf, Glasgow, and are catalogued by the NRAS. Congregations for which records are held include several in Glasgow (Bath Street, Cambridge Street, Glasgow South Side, John Knox Street, John Street, Kelvinside, Portland Street, St George's Place and Whiteinch), as well as Galashiels (Selkirkshire), Grangemouth (Stirlingshire), Ratho (Midlothian) and Tullymet (Perthshire).

Additional registers are held at the NRS, while recent Scottish Baptist yearbooks and directories are available in the ScotlandsPeople Centre's library, with a guide available at **https://tinyurl.com/scottishbaptist**

Catholic Apostolic Church (Irvingites)
This was a church founded in England in 1831, which soon spread worldwide. One of its strongest proponents was Edward Irving, a Scottish Presbyterian minister (later excommunicated by the Church of Scotland) from Dumfriesshire who believed he and others had prophetic powers, and with a strong Calvinist and apocalyptic message. The church was soon organized by him in London under the leadership of a series of 'apostles', all of whom were said to have the gift of prophecy, and tasked with preparing the way for the Second Coming. By the early 1900s there were some twenty-eight congregations in Scotland, but as the last of the apostles died away with no replacements installed and, with the distinct absence of any Second Coming, the church soon declined drastically.

The NRS has a microfilm copy of some baptismal registers for the Catholic Apostolic Church in Broughton Street and East London Street, Edinburgh, catalogued under RH4/174.

Moravians
Initially founded in Bohemia in the fifteenth century, this faith was first established in Ayrshire in 1765, mainly in Ayr but with a congregation in Irvine in the 1770s. Some inscriptions from the Moravian churchyard in Ayr, which took burials from 1771 to 1915, were recorded in *Scottish Notes and Queries*, Volume 11, 3rd series.

The Moravian Church in Britain has an archive in London at **www.moravian.org.uk**

Bereans
A short-lived sect established in Sauchieburn in 1773, which soon spread to Edinburgh and by the 1790s, Glasgow, Stirling, Crieff, Arbroath and Dundee. It died out as a denomination in the mid-nineteenth century. The availability of records is unknown.

Universalists
There have been a couple of Universalist groupings, but the largest was formed as an offshoot of the Relief Church in 1809, with churches in Greenock and Glasgow, Falkirk, Paisley, Johnstone and Ayr. It later identified as part of the Unitarian movement. The availability of records is unknown.

Unitarians

This was first established in Montrose and Dundee in the 1790s, and then spread further to several Central Belt cities and towns, particularly after the formation of the Scottish Unitarian Association in 1813, which was re-formed in 1830. In total, some thirteen congregations were established, of which only four still survive in Aberdeen, Dundee, Glasgow and Edinburgh.

The NRS has records for Edinburgh St Mark's Unitarian Church under CH15, while additional records are noted on the SCAN catalogue for other areas across the country.

For more on the church in general, visit its website at **www.sua.org.uk**

Swedenborgians

This minor sect, also known as the New Church or the New Jerusalemites, was established in Paisley, Glasgow and Edinburgh in the early 1800s, having been brought north from London to a first meeting established in Alloa in 1789. It derives its 'Swedenborgian' name from the writings of its founder in Sweden, Emanuel Swedenborg, who believed he had received divine inspiration from God concerning the establishment of a 'new church', and that he had witnessed the Day of Judgement in the spiritual world.

At least one church continues to worship in Scotland today, based in Paisley (see **www.scotlandschurchestrust.org.uk/church/new-jerusalem-church-paisley**).

Latter-day Saints

The Church of Jesus Christ of Latter-day Saints, also known as the Mormon Church, was first established in Scotland in 1839 by two Scots, Alexander Wright and Samuel Mulliner, who started preaching in Glasgow and Edinburgh.

Today there are several churches across the country, as well as accompanying family history centres at many, with genealogical research a key part of the theological requirement of members. This is done in order to facilitate posthumous baptism of ancestors and to pass 'sealing ordinances', designed to seal family relationships for all eternity. The FamilySearch website provides details on their locations via its home page (p.5).

While FamilySearch is its genealogical records platform, the church's own website for the UK and Ireland is located at **https://lds.org.uk**. A brief history of its Scottish story is found on Wikipedia at **https://**

en.wikipedia.org/wiki/The_Church_of_Jesus_Christ_of_Latter-day_Saints_in_Scotland

The NRS has some correspondence concerning the church's microfilming project of Scottish OPRs, catalogued under GRO5.

Jews

The first Jewish synagogue to open in Scotland was that at Garnethill, Glasgow in 1879, today home to the Scottish Jewish Archives Centre (**www.sjac.org.uk**). Among its holdings is the *Historical Database of Scottish Jewry*, which contains information from the eighteenth century up to the 1920s derived from many sources, such as synagogue, cemetery and naturalization records, documenting well over 16,000 individuals.

The Jewish Genealogical Society of Great Britain at **www.jgsgb.org.uk** is also worth consulting, while an excellent guide detailing a range of Jewish resources, including details of Scottish synagogues and burial grounds, is the revised edition of *Jewish Ancestors? A Guide to Jewish Genealogy in the United Kingdom* by Rosemary Wenzerul (2011, JGSGB Publications).

Sikhs

Sikhs are another relatively recent group to have settled in Scotland, with most having arrived in the late twentieth century. The first gurdwara (the Sikh place of worship) was set up in Glasgow's South Portland Street in the 1920s, and today there are Sikh communities in Glasgow, Edinburgh and Dundee (see **https://scottishsikhs.org**).

However, individual Sikhs have lived in Scotland from the mid-nineteenth century, including Maharajah Duleep Singh, also known as the 'Black Prince of Perthshire', who settled in the county in 1854, and who took up residence temporarily at Castle Menzies where he was famed for his extravagant lifestyle.

For those with Sikh ancestors in Scotland, two useful sites are the Scottish history section of the Sikhs in Scotland website at **www.sikhsinscotland.org/history.phtml** and the cached former Scottish section of the Anglo-Sikh Heritage Trail site at **https://tinyurl.com/scotlandsikhs**

Chapter 5

WHERE WERE THEY?

Chapters 2 to 4 have examined the vital records produced by the state and the churches over the last few centuries. Our primary interest in such items is to find out who was related to whom and how, but of equal benefit is the detail contained within the records about who lived where and when.

These are not the only documents to provide such key information, with a variety of records available that can tell us more about where our ancestors once lived, to tell a story in their own right, and to add further potential layers of understanding to the family narrative.

Census Records
The earliest national census in Scotland was a statistical affair recorded in 1755 by the Reverend Alexander Webster. It noted the numbers of people resident in each parish, broken down further by religious affiliation ('Papist' or 'Protestant'), and by men of fighting age (18 to 56). A published copy of this work is available online at **https://tinyurl. com/1755census**

From 1801, a decennial census has been recorded in Scotland to the present day, with 1941 the only exception due to the Second World War. There were several specific factors behind the establishment of the first census in 1801, chief among them being a desire to understand the size of the population in order to determine the number of mouths that needed to be fed at a time of bad harvests. With the nation also at war with France, another key driver was to establish if there were enough agricultural workers in the country when so many men were serving overseas in the armed forces. From 1801 to 1851 the census was coordinated by the Home Office in London, but from 1861, the Registrar General for Scotland became responsible for the returns north of the border. The records from 1841 and 1851 remained at Westminster until they were returned to Scotland in 1910, to help provide proof of age for those applying for a state pension (for which applicants had to be at least 70 years old), following the establishment of the Old Age Pensions Act in 1908.

The enumeration of the censuses was carried out within registration districts in Scotland, which were initially based on parish boundaries, making it easier to marry up the vital records and the equivalent census entries for a particular area. The number of administrative division types recorded within the censuses increases dramatically between 1841 and 1911; by 1911 there is a wide range of overlapping possibilities, including civil parish and parish ward, ecclesiastical parish or quoad sacra parish, school board district, parliamentary burgh, parliamentary constituency, municipal burgh or police burgh, burgh ward, special water district, special drainage district, special scavenging district, special lighting district and island. Each had a specific purpose, and it is very useful to understand within which boundaries an address lay; for example, it is clearly useful to know the name of the relevant electoral division if you wish to chase electoral registers between the censuses.

From 1801 to 1831 only statistical information for each district was returned to the Home Office, but some enumerations listing people

The censuses from 1851 helpfully note the relationship of those enumerated to the head of the household.

to help prepare these returns have survived in church records and by other means. Details are listed by the NRS at **www.nrscotland.gov.uk/ research/guides/census-records/pre-1841-census-records**

The 1841 census was the first to contain genealogically useful information, with the names of all of those based within a household recorded, and some limited information about their place of birth. From 1851 the records become considerably more useful, noting the relationship of everyone in a household to the 'head' of that household, as well as more detailed information on a parish and county of origin. The 1851 census also notes the exact parish or island of origin in Scotland for those enumerated as well as the county, and was accompanied by a separate census on religious and educational attendance (p.80).

Be careful not to confuse the number in the first column of a census return marked 'Schedule number' for that of a house. This instead refers to the number of the original schedule document which was handed to a householder to fill in on census night and which he or she then returned to the enumerator on the following day. Once the information was copied over to the enumerator's copy, the original schedules were then destroyed. When it comes to addresses, bear in mind also that streets could be renumbered and even renamed between censuses. From 1861, a useful detail on the house itself is recorded for the first time: the number of rooms with one or more windows. This can be extremely useful in understanding the nature of the environment within which your family lived; for example, it is perfectly possible that a family of twelve could be living in a tenement with just two rooms. In each subsequent census, the questions asked evolved further.

For privacy reasons, there is a closure period of 100 years for access to the returns. The 1911 census is currently the most recent available for consultation, with the 1921 Scottish census due for publication in 2021. Although the coverage of the surviving censuses is largely complete, there are some gaps, which are identified by the NRS at **www.nrscotland. gov.uk/research/guides/census-records**

The only website offering online access to the images from the Scottish census from 1841 to 1911 is ScotlandsPeople (**www.scotlandspeople. gov.uk**). For 1881 only, ScotlandsPeople offers an alternative free access to a transcript of the census, as recorded by the LDS Church. Partial transcripts are available for records from 1841 to 1901 on Ancestry and FindmyPast, while FreeCen (**www.freecen.org.uk**) has many transcripts from 1841 and 1851. Scottish Indexes also offers transcripts for many counties within the Borders from 1841 to 1861.

The following is a breakdown of the information found in each of the censuses currently available, with the date of recording noted in brackets.

1841 Census (6 June 1841)
The first of the regular censuses with useful information about individuals recorded the following details:

- The parish name
- Place of residence, usually a village, farm or street
- Whether the house was inhabited or uninhabited
- Age, with males in the left age column, females in the right. In most areas this is rounded down to the nearest multiple of 5 for adults over the age of 15, although some enumerators ignored this instruction and simply recorded the correct age.
- Occupation, or whether of independent means. This was often abbreviated, so a farm servant may be simply noted as F. S., or a handloom weaver as H.L.W.
- Whether born within the county (yes or no), or whether English (E), Irish (I) or Foreign (F).

Unlike subsequent records, no relationships are recorded between different members within a household or marital status.

1851 Census (30 March 1851)
This census identified the parish of birth for an individual, his or her relationship to the head of household, and was also the first to ask for medical details. Within an entry are found:

- The parish, quoad sacra parish, parliamentary burgh, royal burgh, town or village
- Schedule number
- Name of street, place or road, and name or number of house
- Name and surname of each person enumerated within the house on census night
- Relationship to the head of the household
- Condition as to marriage
- Age
- Rank, profession or occupation
- Where born
- Whether blind, deaf or dumb.

1851 Religious and Education Census (30 March 1851)
In addition to the regular decennial census in 1851, there were also two other separate enumerations carried out across Britain on the same

weekend. The first was an educational census, which enumerated details relating to all of the schools in Britain, including Sunday schools. The second was the 'Census of Accommodation and Attendance at Worship', better known as the '1851 Religious Census of Britain'. The purpose of the Religious Census was to ascertain exactly what the religious provision for the country was, and indeed needed to be, at a period following some extraordinary recent developments, including the 1829 Roman Catholic Relief Act, the aftermath of the Irish Famine, and the Disruption of 1843 (p.35).

While most Scottish returns have unfortunately not survived, the report has, and can be found online at **https://tinyurl.com/c7ljoak**, providing a fascinating snapshot of Scotland's ecclesiastical and educational picture of that year.

A small number of records have survived, however. Buried among the kirk session papers for Speymouth, for example, are two printed census forms that have been filled in by hand. The returns are for two congregations: Speymouth, and Garmouth Preaching Station, both in Morayshire, both catalogued by the NRS under CH2/839/20. The information required was as follows:

- Name and description of the church or chapel
- Where situated
- When it first opened for worship
- How, why and by whom it was erected
- The minister's stipend
- The number of free sittings, and those requiring payment
- An estimated number of attendants on 30 March 1851
- Remarks: any further observations in support of the return
- The signature of the minister, elder, session clerk or other duly delegated person to fill out the form.

For Speymouth, we are informed the parish church was opened 'before 1800', and 'when the suppressed parishes of Dipple & Essel (*sic*) were united by decreet of Court of Teinds into one parish named Speymouth, about 1730.' For the minister's salary, the grain stipend due to him was just over £82 and a monetary stipend of just over £53. The glebe was worth £19 and money for the manse was set at £8. Of the church's available seats, only 70 were free, with some 600 other sittings to be leased. On the day of the census 212 members of the congregation attended morning service, and some 18 Sunday Scholars, slightly less than the average number, usually being 280, with 20 scholars. In the remarks section it notes: 'The charge of this parish is a sole one, the present incumbent has only held it for two years byegone; and the stipend is the average for these two years.'

1861 Census (7 April 1861)

This was the first census to be carried out under the authority of the Registrar General for Scotland. It followed the 1851 format but also asked for the following information:

- The number of children attending school between the ages of 5 and 15
- The number of rooms with one or more windows.

1871 Census (2 April 1871)

The boundary details at the top of the page are slightly expanded as follows:

- Civil parish, quoad sacra parish, parliamentary burgh, royal burgh, police burgh, town, village or hamlet.

The following questions were also revised or added:

- Whether deaf and dumb, blind, an imbecile or idiot, or a lunatic
- The number of children attending school between the ages of 5 and 15
- The number of rooms in the property with one or more windows.

1881 Census (3 April 1881)

The question about the number of children at school was removed, and the boundary information at the top of the enumerator's return was again expanded:

- Civil parish, quoad sacra parish, school board district, parliamentary burgh, royal burgh, police burgh, town, village or hamlet.

1891 Census (5 April 1891)

In addition to the information previously required, the boundary information was again revised with additional options to record the names of the parliamentary division, municipal burgh, burgh ward or the name of an island.

The following new information was also required:

- Whether an employer, worker, or working on own account
- Whether able to speak Gaelic (Gàidhlig), or both Gaelic and English.

1901 Census (31 March 1901)
The boundary information now included the name of the police burgh, and a further question was added, asking whether a worker was working at home. The question was no longer asked if someone was an 'idiot'; instead it asked if they were 'feeble-minded'.

1911 Census (2 April 1911)
In 1911, individuals were further asked what their personal occupation was, to which service or industry the worker was connected, whether he or she was an employer, a worker, or working on their own account, and whether working at home. In addition, married women were asked for the duration of their marriage, how many children they had born alive, and how many of those were still living, often referred to as the 'fertility census questions'.

1921 Census (19 June 1921)
In 1921 the fertility census questions from 1911 were removed, as were those questions asking if a person was blind, deaf or dumb. Additional questions asked were:

- A person's age, given in years and completed months
- Whether single, married or divorced if over the age of 15
- If under 15, the status of parents to be given as 'both alive', 'father dead', 'mother dead' or 'both dead'
- Nationality, if born abroad
- If attending school or another educational establishment
- Occupation: trade, employer and place of work
- The number and ages of living children or stepchildren under 16
- An ability to speak Gaelic (Gàidhlig) for those aged 3 or over
- Whether entitled to benefits under the National Insurance (Health) Acts.

National Identity Register
Although no regular census was carried out in the UK in 1941, on 29 September 1939 the National Registration Act 1939 permitted an emergency census to be carried out by the UK government for the purposes of issuing identity cards and a possible list for a personnel draft for the Second World War. The records have survived and are not covered by any formal closure periods (as with the censuses) for they were never officially categorized as a census when the legislation establishing it was passed.

Scottish records are held by the NRS. The purchase of an entry for a named individual is £15 at the time of writing, and if the person of interest did not later die in Scotland, a copy of his or her death certificate needs to be supplied.

As an example of their usefulness, for some time I believed that my great-grandmother Jessie Paton (née MacFarlane) had moved back from Glasgow to Inverness prior to the war. From her National Identity Register entry, however, I discovered that she was still residing at Sunnybank Street in Glasgow, where she was noted as performing 'unpaid domestic duties', and as a widow born on 5 June 1866.

Further information on the register is available at **www.nrscotland.gov. uk/research/guides/national-register**, with information also provided on the earlier registration efforts from 1915, during the First World War, for which records have not survived.

Electoral Registers

Electoral registers can be a very useful tool in identifying adults who resided within a property from year to year, although very few people in Scotland had the right to vote prior to 1832.

Within the burghs, a local council would be drawn from members of the merchant guild and the trade incorporations, but to vote within these elections you had to have a burgess ticket or be a freeman (p.147). The burgh councils in turn would choose their representative to attend Parliament. In the counties, the right to vote was held only by freeholders who held property worth a certain value. Lists of those entitled to vote might be found within sheriff court records at the NRS (p.132).

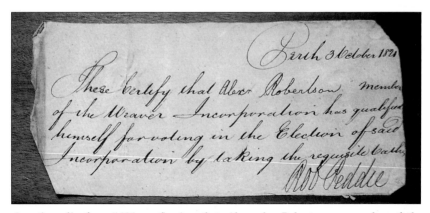

A voting slip from 1821 confirming that Alexander Robertson, a member of the Weavers Incorporation of Perth, had taken the required oath to allow him to vote in the incorporation's elections.

The franchise was extended by the Scottish Reform Act 1832 to permit the vote to male owners of burgh properties worth £10, and property owners of £10 in country seats, or tenants of £50 rental value. This extended the electorate from 4,239 voters in 1820 to 65,000.

Additional reform acts in 1868 and 1884 increased the numbers of males who could vote to some 60 per cent by the late nineteenth century, but for women the struggle took a bit longer. Unmarried women and married women not living with their families gained the right to vote in 1882 for local burgh-based elections only, but it took the First World War and the suffragette campaign to finally see all men and women granted the vote universally from 1918, although with men doing so from aged 21 and women from 30. This again changed in 1928 so that everyone could vote from the age of 21, and once more to 18 and over from 1969. The Scottish Independence Referendum Act of 2013 allowed 16- and 17-year-olds the vote for the first time, with the right subsequently confirmed further in 2015 for all Scottish and local government elections but not UK elections.

Electoral records before 1868 usually consist of poll books, with individuals listed in alphabetical order and recorded details of the property qualification that entitled them to vote. This information was also noted in the new electoral registers from 1872 following the Ballot Act (which first introduced the secret ballot), along with addresses.

From 1918, only the address is given, with entries now grouped by streets within the relevant electoral wards. Electoral wards can sometimes be identified in later street directories, e.g. those for Glasgow and Edinburgh, with the ward number often given after the street addresses in the streets section. There are a few online resources that list trade directories; however, the most notable is the NLS's holdings via the Internet Archive at **https://archive.org/details/nationallibraryofscotland**, which hosts 1,042 street directories and almanacs from 1743 to the mid-1940s.

Electoral registers are held variously in local libraries and at the NLS, with a useful guide to their location being *Electoral Registers 1832– 1948; and Burgess Rolls* by Jeremy Gibson (2008, The Family History Partnership).

The NRS guide on burgh records at **www.nrscotland.gov.uk/research/ guides/burgh-records** notes the voters' rolls within its possession, and their relevant reference numbers; additional burgh registers will be held in local archives across the country. Information on freeholders' records and electoral registers within sheriff court records are detailed at **www. nrscotland.gov.uk/research/guides/sheriff-court-records**

Electoral records for much of Fife from 1832 to 1894 can be accessed on Ancestry, as can returns for the city of Glasgow from 1857 to 1962.

Valuation Rolls

Prior to 1855 valuation rolls were kept on an irregular basis around the country, with few surviving. Following the Lands Valuation (Scotland) Act of 1854 a new annual system was introduced for both burghs and counties which continued until 1989. These recorded the names of the tenant or occupier, and the proprietor, the annual rental value and any other payments owed, as well as the duration of any leases etc.

Each roll covers the financial year following the term day of Whitsun (25 May), and is arranged either by parish or electoral ward, and then by street name and number rather than by a tenant's or proprietor's name. Prior to 1884 the properties listed included the tenants' names only if the annual rental value was worth £4 a year or more, and if their lease was for at least a year in length.

The following records concern my four-times great-uncle William Henderson in Scone, Perthshire as noted in the valuation roll from 1875 to 1876:

Belford Place	
Description	House and garden
Proprietor	William Henderson
Occupied	By proprietor
Yearly rent/value	£5 10s
Feu duty	(none listed)

Belford Place	
Description	House, garden, gig and workshop
Proprietor	William Henderson
Tenant	William Bissett
Yearly rent	£19
Feu duty	£2 payable to Murrayshall

(Valuation Rolls, Scotland. Scone, Perthshire. VR113/21/77. National Records of Scotland)

These show that William was the proprietor of two properties, within one of which he resided and the other leased to William Bissett. Further examination of the rolls before and after this year actually show that he had a different tenant on an almost annual basis. They also note the 'superiority' of the property as residing with Murrayshall Estate, to which the annual 'feu duty' was payable (p.100).

Additional information that may be supplied in the records includes marital condition, occupation, the name of a factor if collecting rent on behalf of a superior, and even solicitors or trustees acting on behalf of a client, particularly if acting on his or her behalf after death.

Most of the valuation rolls have been digitized by the NRS, and can be consulted both there and at the ScotlandsPeople Centre. They have been indexed for every tenth year only at the mid-census intervals, i.e. 1855–56, 1865–66, etc. up to 1915–16, and then for every fifth year up to 1955–56. Many of these rolls and indexes are now also available on the ScotlandsPeople website itself, while the non-indexed collections can be browsed in Edinburgh. Many valuation rolls from 1958 onwards were not microfilmed and must be consulted in their original bound volumes.

Burgh Assessment Rolls

Various other rolls were also recorded for burghs from the mid-nineteenth century onwards listing the values of properties for the purpose of determining local rates. These can act as an alternative if valuation rolls are unavailable.

The following is an example from Glasgow City Archives for a property in the city's Tradeston district in 1904–1905 which was consulted as an alternative to the valuation rolls, these only being available from 1913 onwards at the facility:

Owners assessment 1904–1905 Southern District Vol. 1

Burgh Assessments on Proprietors or Owners for Public Health, Sewage, Roads and Bridges

Section 14 Folio 85

No. of notice	2315
Street	Dale Street
No.	84/82
Proprietors	Glasgow Tramway & Omnibus Co Ltd in Liquidation per Hugh Mayberry, 39 Cambridge Street

Annual value per Valuation Roll £463 Date of payment 8 Dec

(Burgh Assessment rolls 1904–05, Glasgow, Lanarkshire. DCC 10 1/6/148. Glasgow City Archives)

Note that in this case the record shows that the proprietor of the properties has recently been declared bankrupt, with the properties on Dale Street now in liquidation.

Many burgh records, such as for Perth, are held in local archives.

Poor Law Records

Prior to 1845, the Kirk was responsible for the administration of poor relief (p.52). Following the Poor Law (Scotland) Act of 1845, this role was transferred to the state. A system of parochial boards was established in every parish in Scotland, which now reported to a central Board of Supervision in Edinburgh. Poorhouses could be set up independently by a parish in order to treat those who were sick or destitute, or by several adjacent parishes pooling their resources together to form a 'combination workhouse'. The decision on whether or not to admit somebody into a poorhouse, or to give them 'outdoor relief', was now made by an inspector of the poor. Poorhouses were not to be used for the relief of any person able to work, and for applicants denied relief, there was a right to appeal through the sheriff courts (p.132). The system continued to evolve, with parochial boards replaced in 1894 by parish councils and a Local Government Board, with further reforms in 1929 and 1948 passing the system through to local authority control as the welfare state continued to evolve.

Many facts were taken into consideration when administering poor relief, both indoor and outdoor, including the perceived legitimacy of the claim, the feasibility of recouping the expenditure, the moral nature of the applicant, and importantly, whether the applicant had the right of settlement in a parish, which was gained at birth or by five years' residence. In some detailed records, for example, those for Glasgow, you will often find a potted history of every residence within which an applicant has previously lived.

Many Irish and English applicants claiming relief or admission in Scotland were sent back to Ireland or back over the border to England if no source for recompense could be identified; only a medical note could prevent a removal if such a decision was reached. The UK Parliamentary Papers website at **https://parlipapers.proquest.com/parlipapers**, freely accessible through many subscribing libraries, contains detailed letters and annual reports from the second half of the nineteenth century recounting vast lists of people on a parish-by-parish basis who were so returned.

If you cannot access the site, some rolls of people returned to Ireland from Scotland in 1867, 1869 and 1875–1878 are freely accessible at **www.raymondscountydownwebsite.com**. The records are particularly useful in that they identify to which parish in Ireland those being returned were sent back, something not always available in other Scottish records listing Irish folk, such as the census.

The Records
Although the new state-based Poor Law system came into effect in 1845, in some parishes payments continued to be made for a few years during a transitional period (p.52).

A helpful guide available online that can help to target information about the post-1845 poorhouses and the various registers still extant in archives across the country is Peter Higginbotham's website at **www.workhouses.org.uk** (English, Welsh and Irish poorhouses were designated as 'workhouses', as those who found themselves within them could be put to work). This provides a detailed overview of the Poor Law Acts, the locations of former poorhouses, and lists where known records may be held from the institutions, if they have survived. Local archive catalogues, as well as those for SCAN and the NRS, should also be consulted.

Tax Records
Various tax records are held at the NRS which can help with locating a family in a particular parish, as well as provide additional information on a house. The hearth tax records from 1691 to 1695 (catalogued under E69), for example, carry information for those who were taxed simply

because their property had a hearth. Many of the records have not survived, and in some cases only the total number of hearths is recorded per parish, without the names of householders.

The window tax from 1747 to 1798 (E326/1) is a classic example, which noted the names of householders with properties containing seven or more windows. Inhabited house tax from 1778 to 1798 (E326/3) also names householders, alongside the value of their property, while many other taxes can be researched to gain a sense of how wealthy the property-holder was, from male and female servants' taxes, to those imposed on owners of dogs, horses and even clocks.

The surviving records from 1797 to 1798 for farm horse tax tell me that my six-times great-grandfather Andrew Henderson was taxed four shillings for the possession of two horses on his farm in Airntully, Perthshire in 1798. More fundamentally, however, they also help to confirm that he was actually based in Airntully at that point, as was his son, my five-times great-grandfather Peter, who was similarly taxed for his own two horses.

The following tax records are available on ScotlandsPlaces:

- Carriage tax rolls (1785–1798)
- Cart tax rolls (1785–1798)
- Clock and watch tax rolls (1797–1798)
- Consolidated Schedules of Assessed Taxes (1798–1799)
- Dog tax rolls (1797–1798)
- Farm horse tax rolls (1797–1798)
- Female servant tax rolls (1785–1792)

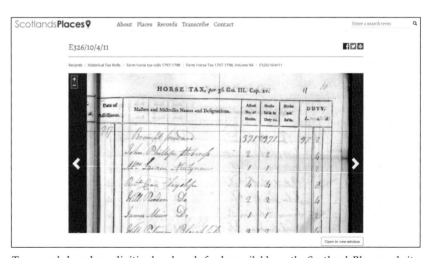

Tax records have been digitized and made freely available on the ScotlandsPlaces website.

- Hearth tax records (1691–1695)
- Horse tax rolls (1785–1798)
- Inhabited house tax (1778–1798)
- Land tax rolls (1645–1831)
- Male servant tax rolls (1777–1798)
- Poll tax rolls (1694–1698)
- Shop tax rolls (1785–1789)
- Window tax (1748–1798)

Inland Revenue Field Books

The NRS-held Inland Revenue Field Books (IRS101-133) were created following the Finance Act of 1910 to help establish the value of land in the country. The books are arranged by parishes and burghs within counties, and by wards within cities. They often include sketched plans and unique details about the properties in question.

A guide to the records is available at **www.nrscotland.gov.uk/ research/guides/inland-revenue-survey-maps-and-field-books**.

Forfeited Estates

Following the rebellions in 1689, 1715 and 1745, various estates were 'escheated' or forfeited from Jacobite supporters by the Crown. The records for these Forfeited or Annexed Estates are contained with the Exchequer records held at the NRS (catalogued under E), and can

The Memorial Cairn at Culloden, erected in 1881 to commemorate the Jacobite fallen of the Forty-Five Rebellion.

contain useful information such as rental rolls and the books of factors charged with collecting rents. Many of the records have been digitized and made accessible through the archive's onsite Virtual Volumes system.

Two published books in particular can be of enormous interest following the 1745 campaign, entitled *Reports on the Annexed Estates 1755–1769* and *Statistics of the Annexed Estates 1755–1756* (both HMSO, 1973). The first carries detailed reports on the make-up of some of the parishes within the estates, with a view to understanding how to improve the lot of the parishioners so that they do not rise up again against the government, while the second provides an effective census for the various estates forfeited, listing the names of the possessors of various farms and statistical details on the people, stock and crops found on each.

Further information can be found on the NRS's Exchequer Records guide at **www.nrscotland.gov.uk/research/guides/exchequer-records**

Maps

Maps can provide a fascinating insight into how your ancestors' environments have changed over the years, particularly when considered in chronological order. Across time, urban growth may have swallowed up particular villages or hamlets, while other settlements might well have disappeared completely, perhaps because of coastal erosion, clearances or abandonment, e.g. the island of Hirta (Hiort in Gaelic) in the St Kilda archipelago to the west of the Outer Hebrides, which was finally abandoned in 1930. Your long-departed house or farm may nevertheless be commemorated by a street name, so it is still worth consulting modern maps.

The best mapping source with which to get started is the fantastic online NLS collection at **https://maps.nls.uk**. This holds thousands of free-to-access digitized images, including those from the Ordnance Survey, formally established from 1791, but going back to the aftermath of the second Jacobite rebellion in Scotland, when the Duke of Cumberland's Map was created by William Roy to help the British army to take control of the Highlands. The records available on the site include the following:

Maps of Scotland, the whole of Scotland, 1560–1928
This contains a series of maps from 1560 to 1928 showing the whole of Britain, from the Scotia: Regno di Scotia map (approx 1558–66) to the Ordnance Survey one-inch maps of Scotland from 1921 to 1928. Also listed is a separate collection of thematically-based maps, showing administrative boundaries, clan territories, geology, railways and roads.

County Maps, maps of Scotland, 1580–1928
A detailed series of maps for each county from 1580 to 1928 presented in chronological order. The section also includes Pont's Maps of Scotland (1580s–1590s), the Blaeu Atlas of Scotland (1654), Herman Moll's County Maps of Scotland (1745), John Thomson's Atlas of Scotland (1832) and J.G. Bartholomew's Survey Atlas of Scotland (1912).

Town Plans and Views plans/views, *1580–1919*
Various maps and surveys of Scottish towns from 1580 to 1919, as well as the maps and reports drawn up for seventy-five towns as part of preparations for the introduction of the Scottish Reform Act of 1832 (p.85), and large-scale Ordnance Survey maps of sixty-two towns from 1847 to 1895.

Series maps of Scotland, 1795–1961
This section predominantly carries Ordnance Survey maps from 1843 to 1991 at various scales. Also included are John Bartholomew & Son's half-inch to the mile maps for Scotland (1926–35) and England and Wales (1919–24), the aforementioned Admiralty Charts (1795–1904), and the post-Second World War Ordnance Survey Air Photo Mosaics of Scotland (1944–1950) collection.

Ordnance Survey maps
This section contains Scottish maps at various scales published by the Ordnance Survey and the War Office from the 1840s to 1960s, as well as collections from England, Wales, Great Britain, Belgium/France and Hong Kong.

Bartholomew maps
This section includes various Scottish maps as produced by Bartholomew & Co., J.G. Bartholomew and John Bartholomew & Son Ltd, from the late nineteenth century to 1940.

Air photo mosaics
Aerial photographs of Scotland taken by the Ordnance Survey between 1944 and 1950, and which can be overlaid by Google Maps and Virtual Earth satellite and map layers for modern comparisons.

Coastal charts Coasts of Scotland on marine charts, 1580–1850
This section includes various marine charts showing the Scottish coast, from Nicolas de Nicolay's 1580 chart *Vraye & exacte description hydrographique des costes maritimes d'Escosse* to John Knox's Map of the Basin of the Tay from 1850. A separate page also lists a series of Admiralty Charts drawn up from 1795–1904 and 1795–1963.

Bathymetrical Survey
This contains a comprehensive examination of 562 inland Scottish lochs, including some 60,000 depths soundings on 223 coloured maps.

Military maps of Scotland (eighteenth century)
This particular section includes a detailed series of maps drawn up by the Board of Ordnance during the Jacobite periods of the eighteenth century, as well as William Roy's Military Survey of Scotland (1747–1755), the immediate forerunner to the Ordnance Survey. The section also hosts Roy's equally detailed map from 1793, Military Antiquities of the Romans in North Britain.

Estate Maps: maps of Scotland, 1772–1878
This small section contains nineteenth-century maps for various estates in Edinburgh, Dumfriesshire, Kirkcudbrightshire, Lanarkshire, Sutherland and Wigtownshire; Edinburgh and a couple in Sutherland from the eighteenth century, for Golspie and Loth (1772) and Assynt (1774).

The NLS Maps Reading Room in Edinburgh, which holds more than 2 million cartographic items, can also be visited, with details available at **www.nls.uk/using-the-library/reading-rooms/maps**

Sites that continue the mapping story to the present day include Streetmap (**www.streetmap.co.uk**) and Google Maps (**http://maps.google.co.uk**). The latter is particularly useful in that it provides a satellite overview image, and a Street View service showing ground-level panoramic photographs. This can be of use if you wish to see what a surviving building looks like today, particularly if you are not in a position to visit.

The NRS has more than 150,000 maps and plans as part of its Register House Plans (RHP) collection, comprising primarily government-based materials but also collections from churches, private organizations, landed estates and families. These include plans of farms, improved estates, feuing plans (p.101), quarries, saltpans and more. Many of the items have been digitized and can be consulted at the facility's General Register House premises on Princes Street, Edinburgh. For items that could not be digitized or which have copyright restrictions, you can make an appointment to visit the organization's Thomas Thomson House facility to consult them there. A guide is available at **www.nrscotland. gov.uk/research/guides/maps-and-plans**

The NRS also has a collection of Ordnance Survey Name Books, catalogued under RH4/23, which were recorded during the creation of the 6-inch and 25-inch scale maps between 1845 and 1878, although not all of the books have survived. Several entries contain additional information on the properties and inhabitants which may be of interest to your research. The books have been digitized and can be found on the ScotlandsPlaces website.

The Statistical Accounts of Scotland

The Statistical Accounts of Scotland were written and published on a national basis on three separate occasions, with the first in the 1790s, the second in the 1830s and early 1840s, and the third over a considerably longer period in the late twentieth century.

The first account, collated by 'Agricultural Sir John Sinclair' runs to some twenty-one volumes; the second, commissioned by the Committee of the Sons and Daughters of the Clergy in 1832 runs to fifteen volumes. In the first account, 938 parish ministers were asked to provide answers to 166 questions concerning their parishes, with 'Statistical missionaries' sent to hurry them on if they fell behind schedule. Among the information returned was the history of an area, the industry, the religious make-up, and from our present point of view, the names of the landholders and estates. The second account maintained this tradition, though in the cities many other observations were also added.

Both accounts are of exceptional value for our research, allowing us a chance to compare the progress of a parish across a gap of approximately fifty years in the midst of one of Scotland's most dynamic periods, incorporating both the Agricultural and Industrial Revolutions.

To give an example of what might be included, let us take a look at the second account for the parish of Forgandenny, which tells us about the parish into which my ancestor Andrew Henderson migrated in 1845 with his son William in order to take up the lease at Mount Stewart Farm (p.135). The account was written in January 1843, just two years before their arrival, and so is fairly contemporaneous. It starts with a description

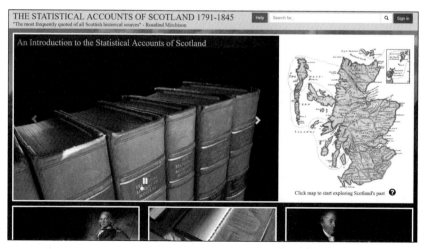

The Statistical Accounts of Scotland provide a snapshot of the country in the 1790s and the 1830s to 1840s.

of the parish itself, telling us that it was 10 miles in length and 2 miles wide and located to the north of the Ochil Hills, with three-quarters of the parish in fact being located there and given over to pasture. Following a brief description of the geology of the parish there then follows a short account of its civil history, including tales from the Covenanters' periods of rebellion in the seventeenth century. We also learn that church records for the parish commenced on 24 September 1654 and were well-kept.

The following section is then particularly handy:

> Land owners: The principal land-owners in the parish are, the Right Honourable Lord Ruthven of Freeland; Lawrence Oliphant, Esq. of Condie; James S. Oliphant, Esq. of Rossie; and Mrs Fechney of Ardargie. With the exception of the barony of Struie, which holds feu of Stirling of Keir, and which formerly belonged to that family, and also of that part of the parish, containing about 1000 acres, which lies in the county of Kinross, and which holds feu of the Grahams of Kinross; the remainder appears to have been divided betwixt the houses of Oliphant and Ruthven, who, during the fourteenth, fifteenth and sixteenth centuries, possessed large estates in this neighbourhood. About three-fourths of the parish still belong to the descendants of these houses.
>
> (*The New Statistical Account of Scotland, Forgandenny, Perth, Vol. 10, Edinburgh: Blackwood and Sons, 1845, p.953*)

Such information can be used to locate contemporary estate records and family papers, if they have survived.

The first two Statistical Accounts collections can be accessed through the University of Edinburgh's EDINA website at **https://stataccscot. edina.ac.uk**. The platform provides an introduction to the collection, and an interactive map to locate parishes and accounts of interest. The accounts are keyword searchable, and you can download and save sections of interest. At the foot of the home page is a link marked 'Related Resources' with additional gems, for example the census of the parish of Stow from 1801. The same accounts have also been digitised and made available through Google Books.

Other Gazetteers

Gazetteers can also provide detailed information on a parish at a particular time in history.

Samuel Lewis's *A Topographical Dictionary of Scotland* from 1846 provides detailed listings for every settlement in Scotland at **www.british-history.**

ac.uk/topographical-dict/scotland. This was compiled on a similar basis to the previous Statistical Accounts, using questionnaires submitted to parish ministers and landed gentry across the country. Among the questions asked were the name of the parish and county where a place was located, on what river or turnpike road it was situated, the name of the nearest post town and distance of the parish from it and the number of acres it comprised. More useful information for the genealogist includes the names of important gentlemen and landowners resident in the area, as well as detailed information on the industry, religion and more of the general population.

In a like manner, Francis Groome's *Ordnance Survey Gazetteer* for Scotland provides similar information, with the 1896 second edition freely available via Electric Scotland (**www.electricscotland.com**).

Additional gazetteers from 1803 to 1901 are also available from the NLS at **https://archive.org/details/scottishgazetteers**

Chapter 6

LAND TENURE

The methods of granting Scottish land ownership and inheriting property are based on Scots Law, through a legal system established from Celtic, Norse, Roman and Norman practices long before the union with England and Wales of 1707, and which has constantly adapted and evolved right up to the twenty-first century.

Scotland
Scotland was never one country from the outset but a series of territories colonized and conquered by various groups, which eventually unified to form a single nation. The Picts, the Gaels, the Angles, the Britons and the Norse all captured and held different areas at various stages, with each group having their own laws and traditions. As the country evolved across time, some regional peculiarities survived.

In the Highlands, land was historically held in the early medieval period through the traditional system known in Gaelic as 'dùthchas', a form of native tenure. The system essentially saw the clans of the region hold on to their respective territories in trust from one generation to the next, with no concept of ownership as understood today.

Further north, within the islands of Orkney and Shetland, a completely different system of land-holding existed in the form of udal law (p.114). These originally formed part of the Norse diaspora, as did part of Caithness on the Scottish mainland, but in 1472 were ceded by the King of Norway to James III in lieu of a failed dowry payment to be paid when the Scottish king married his daughter Margaret four years earlier.

In the Lothians and Borders, the Angles held sway, and later the Northumbrians, while in Strathclyde the Britons were in charge. In time all fused to form the modern nation of Scotland, but the really big changes came following the Norman conquest of England in 1066.

The second Mount Stuart House, on the Isle of Bute, has since 1877 been the seat of the Stuarts of Bute, descendants of Robert the Bruce.

The Normans never conquered Scotland, but from the early twelfth century their influence was certainly brought north of the border through dynastic marriages with nobles of the great Scottish families. The result would see the establishment of some of the major houses and clans, such as the Bruces, the Grahams and the Stewarts, along with one other major import: feudalism.

As a form of land tenure, feudalism moved slowly northwards from the Borders, but it would be centuries before the whole country followed suit, with some parts such as the west Highlands not 'feudalized' until well into the fifteenth century. Concepts such as dùthchas, which had held sway for hundreds of years, were swept away by the superiority of the Crown.

Feudalism

The system of feudalism used in Scotland was effective but takes a little getting used to, enjoying a whole dictionary of legal definitions and words that can make it seem a little more complicated than it often was.

Through feudalism, the entire country was held by the monarch through the Crown, acting as a 'superior' over the land on behalf of God. To exert control, the Crown carved up the country into territories or 'feus' granted to loyal nobles and subjects, who became its dedicated 'vassals'. Each arrangement would be formalized through a charter, a written document which both codified how the land would be used and guaranteed the respective rights of the parties being bound to the agreement. In return for the right of use, a vassal had to pay a 'feu duty' to the Crown, initially through a form of military service, but in time replaced by agricultural produce and labour (via a system known as 'feu ferme'). Later this evolved into a system of financial payments, usually paid once or twice a year at the term days of Whitsun and/or Martinmas.

If a feu was quite small, the landholder simply looked after the property as the Crown's vassal. If the territory was bigger and simply too large to be managed by a single landowner, it could be carved up into smaller, more manageable feus through a process known as 'subinfeudation'. The Crown's vassals would now in turn obtain their own vassals to manage each of these feus on their behalf and act as their superior, much as the Crown did to them. Like the Crown, they could also grant charters to and accept feu duties from the lower rung of vassals beneath them. Sandwiched between the Crown above them and their own vassals below, these middle men were given the special designation of 'subject superiors', or variants such as 'intermediate lawful superiors'.

In turn, the lower-rung vassals beneath these subject superiors could again further divide up the land, unless expressly forbidden to do so. The process could go on until it came to the point where it was impractical to carve up the land any further. Although the vassal, often designated as a 'feuar', could no longer subdivide his or her portion at the bottom rung of this feudal ladder, the land could still be leased out or rented, or some other benefit perhaps derived from it; for example, it could be farmed, or if the plot of land was on one side of a bridge, income could be derived from collecting tolls. As long as a continuous trickle of payments flowed from the bottom of the ladder to the Crown at the top and all were paid their respective dues along the way, just about everybody was happy, with the exception, perhaps, of the humble tenant at the bottom who was simply renting.

These feudal arrangements were granted on a heritable basis. If a vassal died, his or her heir could then inherit the arrangement and continue as the superior's new vassal instead. As land could not be bequeathed in a Scottish will until 1868, there were several unique ways in which this could happen, which will be dealt with further in Chapter 7.

Royal Burghs

From the twelfth century onwards, in order to encourage trade within this feudal system, the Crown created a series of royal burghs in which merchants, craftsmen and tradesmen could manufacture and sell materials with exclusive privileges for national and foreign trade. These burghs were the forerunners of Scotland's modern towns and cities.

As Scotland grew in population, additional lesser types of burgh, ranging from 'burghs of barony' and 'burghs of regality' to 'police burghs' and 'parliamentary burghs', were created by vassals of the Crown, but held fewer privileges. Their records, including those for merchant guilds and trade incorporations (p.147), can provide a wealth of information on your earlier ancestors. Most are held at county record archives, although some remain in private hands, and can be sourced using the SCAN and NRAS catalogues (p.5).

A guide to burgh registers holdings at the NRS is available at **www.nrscotland.gov.uk/research/guides/burgh-records**

Charters

There were various methods by which land could be conveyed, with various charter documents created that acted as formal property deeds.

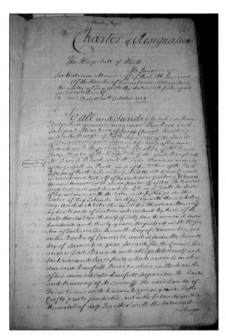

Copy of a charter of recognition granted by King James VI Hospital in Perth in 1759.

If an area of land was carved up into new feus for the first time, an original 'charter of feu' would be recorded for each, defining the areas being made available for new vassals to take possession. They would also include relevant terms and conditions imposed by the superior, including any retained rights of use on his behalf (known as 'dominium directum'), and also guaranteeing certain rights of use for the vassal (known as 'dominium utile'). Once both parties had signed up they were said to be 'infeft' or bound to such arrangements. In such cases, a 'feuing plan' may also exist, a map showing how an area of land was to be carved up into feus and in some cases even noting the names of the original feuars who took possession as the properties became available.

If at any point the vassal broke the agreement, he could lose his right to be infeft and the land or property could be returned to the control of the superior. Similarly, if the superior broke the agreement at his end and perhaps violated the rights of the vassal, the vassal had the right to challenge the transgression or appeal to an appointed body agreeable to both parties to try to resolve the dispute.

If a vassal sold a piece of property to another buyer, the feudal process demanded that the land would first have to be temporarily handed back to the superior (a process described as 'resignation ad favorem'). A new charter was then drawn up for the buyer, who would in turn be confirmed as the superior's new vassal, from which point he or she was then made infeft to the agreement. (If the land was to be returned to the superior permanently, the process was instead described as 'resignation ad remanentiam'.) A new charter would then be granted in favour of the purchaser, either through a 'charter of resignation' or a 'charter of confirmation', and he or she would in turn become the vassal instead of the previous owner. If at any point a charter was issued but needed a subsequent amendment, a 'charter of novodamus' could be granted by way of an update.

Whether through purchase or by inheritance, any new occupant would continue to make the required feu duty payments to his or her superior as part of the deal, essentially for the use of the land on which it was located. As with all conveyances, upon taking entry of the property he or she would also have to pay a 'casualty' to the superior, known as a 'grassum', which was essentially a sum of money to cover certain bureaucratic costs such as the bailie's time and effort. By the nineteenth century a common alternative to this was to simply pay double the annual feu duty at a regular period, such as every nineteenth year.

In most cases charters were similar in what they recorded. There is a general introduction outlining the type of charter, the names of witnesses and the reason for the transfer of land. This is followed by the 'tenendas' clause, outlining the property to be conveyed and the tenure by which it is to be held, and the 'reddendo' clause, outlining the obligations and feu duties to be paid by the vassal to the superior. The document may contain a brief history of the previous transactions tied to the property beforehand. The final part of the charter will then carry an instruction to actually convey the property.

Wonderful as such documents can be, the unfortunate thing for researchers is that charters can often be an absolute nightmare to find.

If a charter was granted by the Crown, things are not too bad in that they were recorded within the Register of the Great Seal of Scotland. Abstracts from these exist for records from 1314 to 1668, and there are indexes to entries from 1668 to 1919, which can be consulted at the NRS. Digitized copies of the Register of the Great Seal of Scotland 1306–1546 and the Register of the Privy Seal of Scotland 1488–1548 (which also includes entries relating to Crown charters) can be purchased and downloaded in e-book format from the Medieval and Early Modern Sources Online (MEMSO) website at **https://tannerritchie.com/memso. php**. The Records of the Parliaments of Scotland to 1707 website at **www. rps.ac.uk** is also worth consulting.

However, for charters granted by subject superiors (i.e. the middle men), it becomes a little more difficult. Some are held at the NRS and others in local archives, while many more have been lost or remain in private hands. There is no central register to such documents, but there is a solution that can thankfully allow you to largely bypass the use of most charters altogether.

Instruments of Sasine

The final part of a charter concerns the actual physical handing over of the property, with the last clause instructing the superior's representatives to draw up a 'precept of sasine' (pronounced 'sayzin'), a written instruction allowing for the actual transfer of the land.

The sasine ceremony was initially a symbolic handing over of a clod of earth or stone by the superior's representative to the new vassal, although there were alternative ceremonies for different communities. From the late sixteenth and early seventeenth centuries the recording of such transfers in dedicated registers instead became the norm (see below). Once the land was taken possession of, the vassal was said to be 'seised' in the property, and the witnessed transaction completed through a written 'instrument of sasine'. The easiest way to find a property transaction is therefore not to look for the charters themselves, but to look for the instrument of sasine confirming the transaction's completion.

Individual sasine instruments can be extraordinarily lengthy, but packed with detail. In addition to noting the basis on which the transaction was conveyed, they will provide a description of where a property was, including a description of which properties existed to the north, south, east and west of it. They can be wonderfully descriptive and may even reveal details about other members of the family should they be involved in the transaction, perhaps as an executor or trustee, or more simply as a witness.

The Registers of Sasines

Prior to the Reformation, the Crown had taken possession of many common lands to which it had no claim, using the process of feudalism to structure their management. In particular, from 1503, James IV catalysed the process with an extensive programme to feu out Crown-held lands.

Nobles also took possession of lands held by the Church of Scotland prior to the Reformation. Illegitimate sons from landowning families were installed into office through corrupt bishoprics, and through them lands were passed into the hands of their families. Indeed, it is sometimes claimed that one of the reasons for the support of the Lords of the Congregation at the Reformation was not just for religious reasons, but to help finish off the job of securing the remaining church lands; a process that actually caused problems for the newly-reformed Kirk as many assets it needed to finance its new programmes of education and discipline were no longer in its hands. A useful book exploring the background to all of this is *The Poor Had No Lawyers: Who Owns Scotland (And How They Got It)* by Andy Wightman (Birlinn Ltd, 2015).

Prior to the sixteenth century instruments of sasines were recorded in 'protocol books' by notaries public. Written in abbreviated Latin, few have survived, although some have been transcribed and published. There were attempts in 1540 and 1587 to create a dedicated register, but it was not until 1599 that the earliest came into existence, in the form of the 'Registers of Sasines and Reversions', better known as the Secretary's Register (after the Scottish Secretary of State). This recorded transactions across seventeen districts in the country (excluding transactions in royal burghs), although records from only seven have survived. The register ceased to be used just ten years later in 1609.

Partly because of the dubious practices in acquiring such lands, an effective law was finally passed to help the nobility legalize their new holdings. The Registration Act and Proscription Act of 1617 introduced the right of 'proscription', which allowed ownership to be recognized for land that had been held for at least forty years without challenge. As a consequence, from 1617 every county was finally required to keep its own individual register.

There were three separate register types within which a transaction could be recorded.

Particular Registers of Sasines

From 1617 to 1868 each county had its own individual Particular Register for transactions occurring within that county only. From 1781 to 1868 these have been entirely indexed through 'sasine abridgements' (p.106), but prior to this the indexing coverage is variable from county to county; the NRS website notes what has been indexed at **www.nrsscotland.gov. uk/research/guides/sasines**

The Particular Registers were largely abolished by a new system in 1868 (below), although a few continued in use up to 1871.

General Register of Sasines
Land transactions from across the country (with the exception of the three Lothian counties) could instead be recorded in the separate Edinburgh-based General Register, which was mainly used if the property transactions being recorded involved land held in more than one county. The General Register has been indexed from 1617 to 1735 and from 1781 to 1868.

The Land Registers (Scotland) Act of 1868 radically transformed the system. The General Register was restructured into a 'New General Register' comprising individual county-based divisions and the Particular Registers were abolished.

Burgh Registers of Sasines
Land held feudally by the country's royal burghs (p.101) under the Crown was said to be so through 'burgage tenure'. The councils of the royal burghs could record transactions within their own dedicated registers, although each burgh commenced registration at different times. Just to make things a bit more complicated, the Burgh Registers usually only contain records for the original medieval part of the royal burgh, known as the 'royalty'.

Burgh Registers survived the 1868 Act, before being finally abolished at various stages in the twentieth century, leaving just the county-based New General Register as the only show in town. Most of the Burgh Registers have been deposited at the NRS (catalogued under B). The exceptions are the registers for Glasgow and pre-1809 registers for Aberdeen and Dundee, which are still held in the relevant local county archives.

NB: For the lesser types of burghs, such as 'burghs of barony', sasine records were mainly kept within the Particular Registers for the county in which they were based.

Locating the Records
NRS and Registers of Scotland (p.4, 109) provide access to post-1868 sasine entries, while the NRS has most earlier sasine registers.

With three possible registers to choose from prior to 1868, it helps to know something of the ancestral geography relating to your forebears. If somebody inherited a property in the parish of Kinclaven in Perthshire, for example, the relevant sasine should most likely be recorded in the Particular Register for Perthshire, but if land was inherited in Kinclaven and perhaps in a neighbouring Fife parish also, this may have instead been recorded within the General Register in Edinburgh. However, if land was inherited in the royal burgh of Perth, then it would almost certainly be recorded within the Burgh Register for Perth. Nevertheless, you might still need to check all three register types.

The Sasine Office entrance at General Register House in Edinburgh, constructed between 1902 and 1904.

Fortunately, a set of digitized abridgements for the Particular and General Registers from 1781 to 1868 has been made available to view on terminals within the NRS. Essentially a short summary of the sasines, they can be searched by surname or place name, and will usually provide enough information to let you know who granted a piece of land to whom, and the arrangement by which it was transferred. A typical example is as follows:

(890) Jul. 2. 1822
MARY KERR, spouse of George McGill residing in Green Street, Kilmarnock, as heir to Margaret Kerr, relict of William Adams, Merchant, New York, her sister, Seised, May 29.1822, – in a House in GREEN of KILMARNOCK with the back ground and House adjoining thereto in the Lane; – on Disp. By Janet Connell and Robert Connell, Shoemaker, Kilmarnock, her husband, to John Aird and Robert Campbell, Merchants there, Jul. 20. 1744; Disp. And Assig. By the said Robert Campbell, to the said John Aird, May 29. 1756; Disp. And Settl., by him, to Trustees, Jan. 6. 1783; Disp. And Assig. By them, to the said Margaret Kerr, Dec.1 1810; and Ret. Gen. Serv. May. 8. 1822 P.R. 147.131

As well as recording that a Mary Kerr became owner ('seised') of the house in 1822, the summary also gives me an entire history of conveyances concerning the property as far back as 1744. It tells me that a John Aird and Robert Campbell obtained it from Janet Connell and Robert Connell following an agreement in 1744, and that John Aird appears to have taken full possession from Robert Campbell in 1756. In 1783 John Aird then placed the future care of the property into the hands of appointed trustees, who in turn conveyed it to Margaret Kerr in 1810. Margaret's sister Mary then inherited the property in 1822, the record also telling us that Margaret had recently passed away and that her husband had already predeceased her by the time of her death. The 'Gen. Serv.' reference at the end notes that Mary proved her right to inherit through a General Service (p.122).

The very final part of the abridgement, 'P.R. 147.131' provides a reference number to the original record in the Particular Register (hence the 'P.R.' prefix). The '147' refers to the volume number from the relevant county's Particular Register collection, and '131' is the page number.

Unfortunately it does not list which county's Particular Register needs to be consulted. In this case, Kilmarnock is in Ayrshire, and so I would need to also source an additional 'sasine code' for that county to complete the reference required to allow me to see the original, which in this case is 'RS14'. Sasine codes for each county are listed in a table at **www.nrscotland.gov.uk/research/guides/sasines**

Knowing this now allows me to consult the digitized record on the archive's Virtual Volumes database. In the search box, typing in the reference 'RS14/147' will load the relevant volume, and I can then scroll along to page 131 to find the precise record.

Pre-1781 Minute Books
Prior to 1781, it gets a bit trickier. Not all of the earlier registers have been indexed, but the archive's online guide shows which have. Digitized microfilm copies of many pre-1781 sasine register indexes are also accessible at local LDS family history centres. If the records have not been indexed, you may need to consult a series of handwritten 'minute books', which offer similar content to the later printed sasine abridgements. Again, these are held at the NRS, but several minute books have also been microfilmed by FamilySearch.

The following is an earlier record concerning John Aird from mid-eighteenth-century Kilmarnock. In the sasine abridgement concerning Mary Kerr found in 1822, it was noted that John Aird came into possession of the property in Green Street following the grant of a disposition or deed by Janet Connell and Robert Connell dated 20 July 1744. The Particular Register of Sasines for Ayrshire prior to 1781 is not indexed, and so I consulted the appropriate minute book. Although the disposition was granted in 1744, there was no sasine recorded at that point. It was not until 1751 in fact that I finally found an entry concerning the property:

30th March 1751
Sea: yeard and house in Kilmarnock

John Aird merchant in Kilmarnock of a little yeard and house thereon in the town of Kilmarnock on a disposition from Janet Connel containing ane infeftment propriis manibus to Ann Campbell spouse of the said John Aird in liferent of the said subject presented by the said Matthew Hopkines

Matt Hopkins William Paterson subs 229 and 230

(Minute Books of the Particular Register of Sasine etc. for the Shire of Ayr, 28 Dec 1744–16 Oct 1756. RS66/4. National Records of Scotland)

This highlights that although a sasine had to be recorded for every transaction, it did not have to be done immediately. This entry in the minute book then allowed me to locate the original document, which provided full details on John Aird's acquisition of the property.

There are some further terms worth defining here. The 'Sea:' prefix before 'yeard and house in Kilmarnock' is just a shortened form of 'seasine' (which often looks like 'seafine' due to the old long-form letter 's' that used to be found in Scottish handwriting). This is just a variant of the word 'sasine'. The abridgement also notes that the sasine agreement contained a document which was 'propriis manibus', a Latin phrase meaning 'in his own hand'. This signifies that John Aird had in this case not bothered with the expense of a bailie, normally employed to perform such a conveyance, but had drawn up the liferent agreement himself.

Liferents and Trusts

In the previous example, John Aird has created a 'liferent' provision for his wife, allowing her use of the property for the rest of her life, and to draw income from it if she chooses by leasing it but not to sell it. Once she has died, it would then pass on to the relevant heir, being heritable property. The full heritable part of the property, i.e. the provision for it to be passed on by inheritance perpetually, was known as the 'fee' (not to be confused with the word 'feu'), so you will often see the term 'in liferent and fee' used in such provisions.

In 1783 John Aird further created a document in which he outlined how the property should be managed following his death. This was a 'trust disposition and deed of settlement' (p.127), in which he nominated his sons and wife to form a trust, with at least two of them coming together to form a quorum to deal with matters concerning the management of his property. Through this method he could ensure that the income derived from the properties could be spread equally between his heirs rather than the property going to a single heir, as demanded at this point by the law in Scotland. For more on Scottish inheritance, see Chapter 7.

A useful glossary of terms relevant to feudal transactions can be found at the Scottish Law Online website at **www.scottishlaw.org.uk/lawscotland/abscotslawland.html**

Registers of Scotland
From 1871 a series of search sheets has continuously recorded sasine abridgements for each particular property, with every new change in ownership added to the relevant sheet with each transaction or inheritance. These search sheets can be consulted at the Registers of Scotland offices in Edinburgh, Scotland, or ordered through its online service at **www.ros.gov.uk** for an appropriate fee. It is also possible to visit the offices to perform searches, or to request research by letter or email. Consult the website for the relevant fees and procedures.

In 1981, another change was brought into the system of recording property transfers, which saw the introduction of a new Registration of Title system, maintained by Registers of Scotland. The New General Register is slowly being phased out as each county gradually transfers into the new system.

Registers of Deeds
Any legal transaction could be copied into a court-held 'Register of Deeds' by agreement between the two interested parties, including those involving property transactions, inheritance, the granting of 'tacks' (leases), bonds issued with land given up as potential security, marriage contracts and more. Locating such deeds is not easy, however, as there were several registers that could potentially cover a jurisdiction, depending on the courts responsible for the area. From 1809 onwards, only the Court of Session, sheriff courts and burgh courts could keep such registers.

For records of the Court of Session (p.137) from 1661 to 1811 consult the 'Books of Council and Session' at the NRS, the main Register of Deeds, which were kept by three separate clerks' offices. The office of Dalrymple is catalogued as RD2, Durie as RD3 and Mackenzie as RD4. From 1812 there was a single office dealing with such deeds, with its records catalogued under RD5. There are various annual indexes available, and at the time of writing, indexes for the three series from 1661 to 1769 are also being produced by Scottish Indexes. If a deed has not survived, a document called a 'warrant' may well have (the original document signed by the parties before registration). Further information on these is available at **www.nrscotland.gov.uk/research/guides/deeds**

A useful example lies with a marriage contract from March 1881 which was recorded in the Register of Deeds the following month. This was between a Thomas Law, shipbroker in Glasgow, and Helen Henderson, daughter of James Henderson, Superintendent Inspector of Factories for Scotland, who resided in Pollokshields. The details from the 1881 index were as follows:

Granter	Thomas Law, shipbroker, Glasgow
Grantee	Helen Henderson
Deed	Marr Con.
Date	22 MAR 1881
Registered	28 APR 1881
Details	Vol. 1808 Fol. 262 MB 136

(Register of Deeds, Scotland. 1881 index. LAW, Thomas. National Records of Scotland)

The prenuptial contract outlined which of his possessions would go to Helen following his death, a £300 payment for her mourning garments, and a regular annuity of £300 to be paid to her in two half-yearly payments, to be reduced to £100 if she remarried. Thomas also outlined provisions for any prospective children to be produced from their marriage, and a quorum of trustees to oversee a trust to do so, listing the financial assets to be used for their benefit and that of his widow. Note that the indexes are indexed alphabetically by the grantor's name only, in this case Thomas.

Equivalent Registers of Deeds from the sheriff courts (p.132) are held at the NRS also, with the exception being those for Orkney and Shetland, which are held in the respective county repositories. For burgh courts, some are held in local archives and others at the NRS. A good example of these is for the burgh of Perth from 1566 to 1811, which has been digitized and made available on Ancestry.co.uk. This comprises the 'Registers of

Acts and Obligations from 1599–1805' (with gaps), and the 'Register of Deeds' from 1658 to 1666 and 1787 to 1811.

There were additional Registers of Deeds kept by the lower courts, such as franchise courts (p.145), as well as the Commissary Court (p.144). Hunting for deeds can be painful, but often rewarding.

Estate Papers

Not all of our ancestors owned land, with those of the labouring classes, such as agricultural workers, weavers or coal-miners instead renting properties from an individual, an estate or a burgh, often with little security of tenure. Tracing where they were prior to the 1841 census may involve locating them in sources such as parish records, but another set of records worth trying to locate are estate papers, which may provide information on the rents or feu duties that they had to pay, or any tacks (leases) that they may have held.

To identify the landowner for the area within which you are interested, it is first worth consulting the Statistical Accounts of Scotland (see p.95), which in most cases will list the principal superiors within each parish. By identifying which family or individual held a particular area you can then begin to search for the relevant records, which may be at the NRS, at a local archive or within private hands, assuming they have survived.

The NRS holds many records at Edinburgh from estates among its Gifts and Deposits collection (GD), with particularly good examples including the Breadalbane Muniments (GD112) and the Grandtully Muniments (GD237) for Perthshire. As these are deemed to be private records held in the care of the archive, you will be allowed to consult them but not to photograph them with a digital camera, these being one of the few sets of records for which permission is not given. Other records of use at the NRS can be found with the RH9 and RH11 series and the CR series (Commissioners of Crown Estates).

The following is an example of a rental payment made by a relative who lived in Airntully, parish of Kinclaven, Perthshire:

Perth: Rental of the baronies of Strathbraan, Murthly and Airntully dated 1801

John Henderson crop 1801
Entry 1793
Endurance 19
Expiration 1812
Coals 4 bolls 4 hens
£26 13s 5d

(Miscellaneous Papers. Scotland. 1801. Perth: Rental of the baronies of Strathbraan, Murthly and Airntully. CR4/23. National Records of Scotland)

In addition to detailing his annual rent, this record from 1801 notes that John had a nineteen-year lease which he entered into in 1793 and which was due to expire in 1812.

Rental rolls can tell you where someone was at any point, but they can often add a little more detail about the area where your ancestors lived.

My four-times great-grandfather William Paton was born in Sconieburn, within the Perthshire parish of Perth. His father John Paton was a weaver who by the late 1790s had moved the family to an area called Carr's Croft on the outskirts of the city. William, like his father, became a handloom weaver, and following his father's death in 1820 he continued to reside at Carr's Croft, where he was recorded in the 1841 census, with his brother John, also a weaver, noted as one of his neighbours. William eventually passed away on 28 February 1849, not at Carr's Croft but at Scott Street within the burgh.

I was able to locate a rental book in Perth, held by King James VI Hospital in the city, which included Carr's Croft and covered the period from 1847 to 1865. For the previous fifty years the cottages there had been held on a tack from the hospital by the Weavers Incorporation of

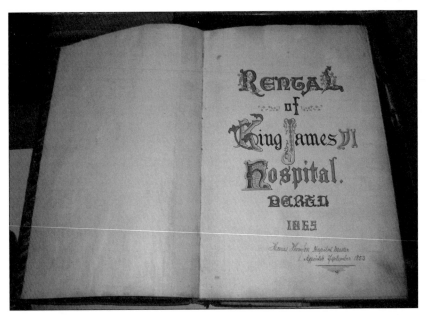

One of the beautifully-illustrated rental books from King James VI Hospital in Perth.

Carr's Croft, Perth, home to the author's Paton ancestors from the 1790s to the 1840s.

Perth, which had allowed them to fall into a complete state of disrepair, no doubt because of the virtual collapse of the handloom weaving industry in the burgh within this period. When the properties returned to the hospital's control (a process called 'reversion'), it initially did little to improve them.

In 1853, a note beside No. 2 Carr's Croft stated that it was unlet by 1856, with 'the tenement in ruins', while the house at No. 4, previously occupied by William Paton's brother John until July 1850, was also described as 'in ruins'. At No. 9, things were not much better, with a note stating 'House in bad order and rent not paid', and a further note in 1858 recording how 'one half of the above is unlet as untenantable before repairs'. The tenant at No. 14 had been 'bedrid all the time he occupied, and never was able to pay any rent', while at No. 18, 'this tenement fell one stormy night in November 1848'. Although William himself had moved away by this point, it is perhaps not difficult to see why.

Tacksmen

In Highland society, clan chiefs would lease large portions of land to kinsmen, often through a heritable arrangement that lasted for generations. The relations would hold on to some of the land for their own use and would lease out portions to subtenants beneath them. As well as their role in land management, they also had a military role within the clan, acting as captains and lieutenants to their chiefs. In

Gaelic each of these relations was known as a 'fear-taic', or 'tacksman' in English.

With the land reforms introduced via the Highland Clearances of the seventeenth to the nineteenth centuries and in the aftermath of the various Jacobite rebellions, the role of the tacksman became redundant. Many were soon forced to emigrate, and often encouraged their subtenants to emigrate with them. A good example was John MacDonald of Glenaladale. Aggrieved at changes being implemented on the Clanranald estates, MacDonald helped 200 of his former tenants to emigrate to Prince Edward Island in 1772, with financial assistance from the Scottish Catholic Church.

The End of Feudalism

One of the failings of feudalism was that when a charter stated the amount of a particular feu duty to be paid to the superior, that charge still remained the same in all future transactions. The value of one pound sterling as a feu duty in 1750 was considerably greater than the value of one pound sterling in 2000. Inflation was not taken into account, and for many superiors the cost of a stamp to post a request for the payment of duties eventually became worth more than the actual revenue that could be recovered.

Feudalism ultimately ended in Scotland through the Abolition of Feudal Tenure (Scotland) Act 2000, as enacted from November 2004.

Udal Tenure

While feudalism historically dominated land ownership in Scotland, it was not the only form of tenure. The Church of Scotland, for example, did not hold its land as a vassal of the Crown, but instead owned its property outright through a non-feudal form of possession called 'allodial tenure', with land said to be held absolutely 'in allodium'.

In Orkney and Shetland land was held from the seventh century through a form of allodial tenure called 'udal tenure', which existed within the islands as a direct result of their former existence as a holding of Norway (p.98). Under the old Norse Law, land became held by udal tenure after having been inherited by the fourth generation of a family, following continuous previous ownership by a person's father, grandfather and great-grandfather. If land held udally was to be sold, it could only be so conveyed with the agreement of other members of the family, or following a period where other members could first try to redeem the lands themselves.

Various conditions existed within this system to protect a family's interests. For example, if udal land was sold outside of the family, a member of the family could redeem it within twenty years by making a public announcement that they had submitted a claim to the Thing (the Norse parliament), with the purchase price then set at 80 per cent of the value of the property. The right was only forfeited after it had remained outside of the family's possession for a continuous period of sixty years.

Following Scotland's acquisition of the islands in the fifteenth century, attempts were made to impose feudalism and to make the landholdings subject to the Crown, but udal tenure doggedly remained. Those who held land outright were known as 'udallers'. Although there were no feudal restrictions on how they sold or disposed of their lands, or any obligations to pay an annual feu-duty, udallers did have to pay a form of tribute directly to the Crown each year called 'skat', which was not abolished until 2004.

Having never been formally superseded by Scots Law, udal tenure still exists in the islands, although to a much lesser extent. An interesting article on the history of the udal system in Orkney and Shetland by William Jardine Dobey, including information about inheritance through the udal system, is found at **https://tinyurl.com/UdalLaw**, while *The Law of Succession* by Sir Iain Moncrieffe (2009, John Donald / Birlinn) discusses the similarities between this form of tenure and older Celtic forms of land-holding.

Other Forms of Tenure

There were also some other peculiar arrangements to be found within pockets across Scotland, such as the Four Towns of Lochmaben in Dumfriesshire, these being the villages of Hightae, Greenhill, Heck and Smallholm within Lochmaben parish. Property here was also held outright through udal tenure by the 'King's rentallers' or 'the King's kindly tenants', through a form of perpetual hereditary lease. As a consequence, any time a property changed hands it was not entered into the sasine register but via a deed of conveyance in the viscount's rental rolls. Kirkyetholm in Dumfriesshire also had 'kindly tenants' in residence.

'Tenancy at will' was another way that land could be held, whereby a tenant rented land from a landowner, upon which he could then build a house. Rent was payable, but if the tenant failed to pay the rent he could be evicted. No title deed was ever issued in the process, making it very informal. It was commonly found on the north-east coast and in various highland villages.

A further form of holding was 'leasehold', where the property was owned for a stated period, often for hundreds of years. As it was technically a form of tenancy a small sum called 'ground rent' was collected annually, but which often amounted to a very small token amount. Leaseholds are found all over Scotland, being most prevalent in parts of Lanarkshire, but also in Strathaven, Blairgowrie, Ullapool and Montrose. On 28 November 2015, the Long Leases (Scotland) Act 2012 converted the leases of properties at least 175 years in length into ownership if they still had 100 years left to run and attracted an annual rent of less than £100.

One community in Scotland which fought long and hard for better security of tenure was the crofters of the Highlands and Islands, who owned small agricultural holdings on which they could barely scratch a living from the soil and who were badly affected by the Clearances of the nineteenth century.

If your ancestor was a crofter, a useful resource is the crofting section of the Am Baile website at **www.ambaile.org.uk** which includes the *Crofter* newspaper from the 1880s, while the four-volume Napier Commission of 1884, which investigated the grievances of the crofting community across the north of Scotland, can be read online at the Lochaber College website at **www.whc.uhi.ac.uk/research/napier-commission**

Chapter 7

INHERITANCE

When a person died within Scotland, the assets he or she left behind were categorized within two forms of estate, 'moveable estate' and 'heritable estate', both of which were disposed of through very different procedures before 1868. Records of inheritance can provide a range of genealogical clues about a family, as well as convey a sense of its social status.

In this chapter we will look at how inheritance worked in Scotland, and the records that were generated.

Moveable Estate
This was the term for the deceased's possessions that were not pinned down: the bedding, the cash stuffed under a floorboard or in a bank account, etc.

Traditionally, when a man died, his spouse was automatically entitled to a third of his possessions (the widow's part or 'jus relictae'), and his children another third (the bairns' part, or 'legitim'). Only the final third could be bequeathed as he saw fit ('the deid's part'), which then went through the 'confirmation' process (see below).

As the eldest son usually got to inherit the deceased's heritable property (p.120), he was not entitled to a share of the legitim, and as such may not be mentioned in the deceased's will for that reason. However, he could be entitled to possessions relevant to the operation of his heritable holding, for example a plough on a farm, with such possessions known as 'heirship moveables'.

Note that although suicide (legally called 'self-murder' in Scotland) was never a crime in Scotland, the moveable estate of a person deemed to have killed himself or herself could be made 'escheat' (forfeit) in an action taken at the Court of Session (p.137) by the Crown's agents against the deceased's executors. A defence against this was to prove that the deceased had been insane when attempting to carry out the act.

Testaments

During his or her lifetime, the deceased may have written a will, or set up a trust disposition and settlement prior to 1868 (p.127), with such documents potentially registered within a court's Register of Deeds (p.109). If the deceased made a revision to his or her will before death, it could be appended as a 'codicil'. Whether the deceased had recorded a will or not, the final conveyance of his or her possessions was formalized through a civil-based commissary court (p.144) before the mid-1820s, or through a sheriff court (p.132) thereafter. Through this process, called 'confirmation', any will would be identified, an inventory carried out of the deceased's possessions, and the relevant executors appointed by the court to administer the estate.

The documents outlining the confirmation procedures were known as 'testaments'. If a person was 'testate' (i.e. left a will), the record of confirmation was known as a 'testament testamentar', but if the deceased was 'intestate' (with no will) the record generated was called a 'testament dative'. If following the completion of the confirmation process further estate was then located, it could also be confirmed subsequently, with the document generated known as an 'eik'.

A good example of why it pays to consult all relevant probate documents lies with the will of my five-times great-uncle, Dr William Henderson, who died aged 86 in Perth on 19 October 1870, without issue. On 28 May 1870 William had set up a trust disposition and deed of settlement in order to lay out his requests for the disposal of all of his estate, both heritable and moveable, and appointed four trustees to act as his executors. These included his favourite nephew, also called William, to whom he bequeathed £1,000. The physician also wished for a charitable fund for the poor to be established, called Doctor William Henderson's Mortification, to be overseen by his executors, and in his will, further described in some detail which of his possessions should go to whom.

A week later, on 6 June 1870, Dr Henderson suddenly revised his wishes with a codicil. He removed his nephew William as a trustee, and reduced his legacy from £1,000 to £600. The reason is not clear, but his nephew was the owner of Mount Stewart Farm (p.135), where his niece Janet had been murdered in 1866. Young William eventually died insane in an asylum in Scone in 1890, and it may well be that his uncle had some insight into his nephew's deteriorating state of mind.

When Dr Henderson subsequently died in October 1870, his will and codicil were subjected to the confirmation process and an inventory drawn up. This itemized his business dealings, including a loan to a friend in Canada, various investments with the rapidly-developing railway companies, the gas company in Perth, and even the Perth Wheaten Bread Society. His total assets were worth almost £20,000, making him a late-nineteenth-century equivalent of a modern millionaire.

Accessing Testaments

All surviving court testaments can be found from the mid-sixteenth century to 1925 on ScotlandsPeople. A guide to the records, with detailed examples, is available at **www.scotlandspeople.gov.uk/guides/wills-and-testaments**. Most records confirm estates left in Scotland, but it was possible to have copies of overseas probate documents 'resealed' through the Scottish courts from 1858 if there was a Scottish interest among the deceased's holdings. As such, even if your ancestor emigrated, it is still worth consulting ScotlandsPeople. Prior to 1858, confirmation of Scottish property owned by residents overseas or elsewhere in the UK was handled by the Edinburgh Commissary Court (p.144).

Confirmation records for later years are held at the NRS, with information on their accession available at **www.nrscotland.gov.uk/research/guides/wills-and-testaments**. Note that the most recent wills for the last ten years are still retained at the relevant sheriff courts; to access these you will need to write to the Commissary Department, Edinburgh Sheriff Court, 27 Chambers Street, Edinburgh EH1 1LB.

Calendars of Confirmations and Inventories

Following the Sheriff Courts (Scotland) Act of 1876, a series of books was published annually by the commissary clerk in Edinburgh from 1877 to 1959, known as the *Calendars of Confirmations and Inventories*. These contain basic annual summaries of all confirmations made in Scotland, indexed by the name of the deceased, and with women indexed under their married names. They note the deceased's name, date and place of death, whether they died testate or intestate, the value of their estate, the date on which confirmation was made, and at which sheriff court. From 1921 there were two volumes a year, the first containing entries for all surnames beginning with the letters A to L, the second from M to Z.

The following is the calendar entry for my great-grandfather David Hepburn Paton, who died in Brussels in 1916:

PATON, David Hepburn, Shop manager to R & J Dick Ltd, late of Rue St. Catherine, Brussels, Belgium, formerly of 100 Cumberland Street, Glasgow, died 12 March 1916 at Brussels, intestate. Confirmation granted at Glasgow, 25 February, to Jessie McFarlane or Paton, 18 Aitken Street, Dennistoun, Glasgow, Executrix dative qua relict. Value of estate £204 17s 1d.

(Confirmations, Scotland. 25 February 1919. PATON, David Hepburn. Calendar of Confirmations and Inventories. 1919)

The author's great-grandfather, David Hepburn Paton, from Blackford, Perthshire, was a civilian shopkeeper in Brussels. He died from an illness in 1916, after spending over a year in hiding to avoid internment.

In this instance David died without a will, and his personal estate was not transferred until three years after his death, mainly because his wife and family had remained trapped as civilians in occupied Brussels for the rest of the war.

Many local records offices and libraries have copies of these calendars. The NRS hosts digitized copies from 1901 to 1959 in its Historic Search Room computers, while Ancestry has digitized most as its 'Scotland, National Probate Index (Calendar of Confirmations and Inventories), 1876–1936' collection.

Heritable Estate

Heritable estate was the part of the deceased's possessions that was very firmly pinned down, such as a house or portion of land, but it also included coats of arms, which were treated as if they were property (p.149). Heritable estate could not be left in a will in Scotland until 1868, and instead had to be conveyed through a separate process.

Following a person's death in Scotland a prospective heir could not simply just assume full ownership of the deceased's heritable estate, but instead had to go through a formal recognition process. Until formally inherited, the unclaimed estate was said to be in a legal void known as 'in haereditas jacens', and the claimant was an 'apparent heir', a designation which stayed from the time of the previous owner's decease until the point when he or she was legally recognized as the new owner. A person had a year and a day to decide if they wished to put themselves forward as the apparent heir, with this period known in Latin as the 'annus deliberandi' or 'tempus deliberandi'. Not everybody wished to go through with it, especially if the deceased left serious debts behind for which the heir could then become liable.

If an ancestor left an estate burdened with debt, there was a legal means by which the apparent heir could limit any liabilities for this debt before taking up possession of the estate through the formal inheritance process. This was to take possession of the property 'cum beneficio inventarii', i.e. with the benefit of an inventory. An inventory would be drawn up detailing the extent and value of the estate, which had to be lodged with the sheriff-clerk of the relevant county within a year of the ancestor's death. Although the heir would still be liable for a predecessor's debts, he or she would only now be liable to the extent of the inventory's value, with the debt also now attached to the heir, and not to the estate itself, i.e. it could not be further passed on to his or her descendants in due course.

Whether an apparent heir took informal possession or not, the problem remained that he or she could not pass on the property further unless he or she had completed the inheritance process. To do this various hoops had to be jumped through, but the process for doing so was very much dependent on the type of feudal superior (p.99) with responsibility over the property in question.

There were two main ways by which such recognition could be carried out: a) the 'services of heirs', or b) through the issue of a 'precept of clare constat'.

The Services of Heirs

If the land in question was held of the Crown, the process prior to 1847 involved the apparent heir first purchasing a type of warrant called a 'brieve' from the Scottish Chancery, which contained a mandate for a judge to call a jury together to form an inquest into his or her claim. The jury would meet fifteen days after the brieve had been publicly proclaimed in the area where its members were to meet, with its role to then establish both the extent of the land or property in question and to confirm whether the candidate before them had a legitimate claim. Often the jury would actually have a member of the family included to help the procedure.

If the apparent heir was who he or she said they were, the jury would find in their favour and the decision would be sent to the Scottish Chancery via a document called a 'retour'. At this point an instruction would be given for the judge to issue a sasine (p.103) to formally complete the process, at which point the apparent heir was no longer in any way apparent, but very much the actual owner. The system was changed in November 1847 so that brieves no longer required to be purchased, and a simple petition to the county sheriff, or the newly-created post of Sheriff of Chancery, was all that was now needed to kick-start the process.

There were two main types of retours, known as 'special services' (or 'special retours') and 'general services' (or 'general retours'). They were written in Latin and could be quite lengthy.

Special services tended to deal with any properties where the ancestor had been infeft to the Crown (see p.101), and his titles previously confirmed by a sasine or sasines. For example, if the heir's father had inherited an area of land which had an associated charter granted and which had been conveyed to him by a sasine, then he would have been infeft to that agreement, and so his heir in turn would need to inherit via a special service. The judge convening the jury in this case would be the sheriff of the county.

The jury would ask for proof of the deceased's death, proof that the apparent heir was entitled to inherit (which could involve witnesses giving testimony), the name of the superior from whom the lands were held by the deceased as a vassal, the form of tenure, and the extent or value of the land determined, in order to establish what the casualty for entry to the property would be (p.102). The valuation was actually determined in two ways: the 'auld extent' was based on the value given in older retours, and the 'new extent' given by the value recorded in more contemporary county cess (land tax) books.

A general service was a simpler document that merely confirmed the apparent heir's identity. General services proceedings could be heard by any magistrate, and were much more basic affairs, with the apparent heir simply asked for proof of the deceased's death, and proof that he or she was the heir.

Judgements passed by the courts were open to challenge for forty years, and if a more legitimate and closer heir was discovered or stepped forward with a claim, the original service could be invalidated and a new one granted in favour of the true lawful heir.

There are published abridgements to help locate the relevant records of services passed by the courts. The first collection, covering the period from 1544 to 1699, is known as the *Inquisitionum ad Capellam Domini Regis Retornatarum quae in Publicis Archivis Scotiae adhuc Servantur, Abbreviatio*. As the title suggests, these are recorded in Latin, although a small number of entries are recorded in English in the mid-seventeenth century during Cromwell's Commonwealth period. The collection is not quite complete,

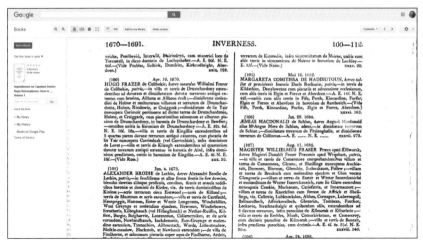

The three volumes of the Inquisitionum ad Capellam Domini Regis Retornatarum are freely available on Google Books.

with entries missing from 1611 to 1614, and there are also a few entries missing throughout the run simply because they were never retoured to the Chancery. Some of these unreturned services may be found in sheriff court records, or in the records of some of the lesser courts.

The abridgements come in three volumes, with the special services presented chronologically in order, county by county, while those for the general services are all lumped together in one big national chronology. Despite the language difficulty, the pain is eased somewhat by the fact that they are thankfully indexed both by surname ('index nominum') and by place ('index locorum').

The special services are abridged in Volume 1 (Aberdeen to Kirkcudbright) and Volume 2 (Lanark to Wigton), while the general services are abridged in Volume 2; the indexes for both types are located in Volume 3. This third volume also has indexes for appointments of tutors to those inheriting in their minority ('brieves of tutory'), or those not sound of mind ('brieves of idiotry' or 'of furiosity'), which together form the *Inquisitiones de Tutela*.

The following is an abridgement example from a retour of special services:

(355) Jan. 10. 1699

GULIELMUS HAIRSTANES de Craigs, haeres Mathei Hairstanes de Craigs, patris, – in 10 libratis terrarum de Over Kellwood, infra parochiam de Dumfries; – terris de Nether Kellwood infra dictam

parochiam; – terris de Bonnerlands infra parochiam de Carlavrock. – A.E. 20l. N.E. 60l.
xlvii. 899.

(Retours, Scotland. 10 January 1699. HAIRSTANES, Guilelmus. *Inquisitionum ad Capellam Domini Regis Retornatarum*, Vol. 1. Inquisitiones Speciales, Dumfries. 1811, Record Commission)

Even if one has little or no Latin, it is still possible to get the general sense of this. The abridgement basically states that William (Gulielmus) Hairstanes of Craigs is the heir (haeres) of Matthew Hairstanes of Craigs, and that he is inheriting land (terris) in Over Kellwood and Nether Kellwood within the parish (infra parochiam) of Dumfries, as well as Bonnerlands in the parish of Carlaverock. The part containing A.E. 20l means Auld (Old) Extent 20 pounds, and N.E. 60l means New Extent 60 pounds. The final reference is for the original retour document, being volume and page numbers.

The style of these special services compares markedly with the much more basic general services entries:

(675) Feb. 11. 1617
JONETA COCHRANE, haeres Patricii Cochrane mercatoris ac burgensis de Edinburgh, fratris.
vi.253

(Retours, Scotland. 11 February 1617. COCHRANE, Joneta. *Inquisitionum ad Capellam Domini Regis Retornatarum*, Vol. 2. Inquisitiones Generalis, entry 675. 1811, London, Record Commission)

In this entry, Janet Cochrane is identified as heir to her brother Patrick Cochrane, a burgess and merchant in Edinburgh. Note that surnames and place names are not Latinized in any way, making them easy to find when consulting the name and place indexes in Volume 3.

The abridgement records are freely found on Google Books (Volume 1 **https://tinyurl.com/Retours1**, Volume 2 **https://tinyurl.com/Retours2**, and Volume 3 **https://tinyurl.com/Retours3**). Printed copies are also held within various libraries and at the NRS.

Decennial indexes for retours from 1700 to 1859 are available at the NRS, and are also freely available on FamilySearch at **www.familysearch.org/search/catalog/1004156?availability=Family%20History%20Library**. These abridgements are written in English, but both special and general services are now listed together. There are again two separate lists, the Main Index and an accompanying Supplement.

The records are indexed alphabetically in periods of ten years, starting with 1700–1709, 1710–1719 and so on. All heirs are found in the main index, with the following an example:

Name of the Person Served	Hunter – Helen – (or Colston)
Distinguishing Particulars	Wife of William Colston in Gifford, to her Uncle Andrew Hunter, Feuar there – Heir General – 22d January 1754
Date of Recording	1754 April 16
Monthly No. 16	

If you wish to find the name of the heir to a particular ancestor who has a different surname to the deceased, you will need to consult the supplement that accompanies each decennial listing, which acts as a finding aid. A typical example would be:

Names of the Persons served to, by Heirs not bearing the same Names

Stevenson – John – Wright, Kilsyth

Names of the Heirs – which see in the Principal Index
Renny – Jean – (or Gillies) – (Heir of Provision General)

Having found the name of the ancestor John Stevenson, I would now need to go back to the original index and look up Jean Renny's entry for the details recorded for her relevant retour.

The indexes continued beyond 1859 up to the mid-twentieth century (as annual indexes, rather than decennial), which can be viewed at the NRS. In the index for 1906 there are five pages of additional entries recorded for the period 1700–1859 which were originally missed. Other entries may be found in local court books where the record has not been retoured to the Chancery.

Precepts of Clare Constat
Services of heirs were usually recorded when the feudal superior was the Crown, or for those seeking proof of identity. If, however, the land was held of a subject superior (p.100), you did not need to go through the Services process, and could instead simply obtain a document from him

that showed that he or she recognized that you were the lawful heir. This document was colloquially known as a 'precept of clare constat', and named the heir and details of the property to which he or she wished to inherit.

There is no centralized register of such documents, which may be found within estate papers, dusty cellars and solicitors' offices, assuming they have survived at all. However, whenever land was transferred, whether by purchase or by inheritance, it had to be entered into a Register of Sasines (p.104), and it is here that you will find evidence of such a transaction. The following is an example:

MARION McKECHNIE, spouse of Hugh Paton, Grocer, Largs, as heir to John McKECHNIE, Grocer and Manufacturer there, her father, Seised, in the half of a Dwelling House with Byre and Yard at the back thereof on the north side of the Street of LARGS, and of a Barn extending to about 10 Feet in length adjoining, par. Largs; on Pr. Cl. Con. By Gen. Sir Thomas Makdougall Brisbane of Makerstoun and Brisbane, Sept. 21. 1849. P. R. 353.249.

Although vassals of subject superiors did not usually need to go through the services process, occasionally an apparent heir might have had to do so additionally in order to obtain proof of identity before obtaining a precept of clare constat, in cases where it was not always clear to a subject superior that the claimant was who he or she said they were, as an extra form of security or proof. As such, it is sometimes possible to find claimants having gone through both processes. In the above example, Marion McKechnie did exactly that, with her entry in the services of heirs index as follows:

Named of the Person Served	Paton – Marion – (or McKechnie)
Distinguishing Particulars	Wife of H. Paton, Grocer in Largs, to her father, John McKechnie, Weaver there – Heir General – 6th October 1849
Date of Recording	1849 Oct. 12
Monthly No. 10	

An interesting point here is that the sasine abridgement notes her father as a grocer and manufacturer, whereas the services index notes him as a weaver. It is always worth looking for a services entry in the index even if the sasine shows entry was by a precept of clare constat, as you may find some additional information.

As with services of heirs, inheritance via a precept of clare constat was open to challenge by anyone claiming to have a better claim, although in this case only within a period of twenty years after the original apparent heir inherited.

Trust Dispositions and Settlements

Although land could not be conveyed through a will prior to 1868, there was a process through which the deceased could posthumously convey heritable property to whomever he liked in order to bypass the rules of primogeniture.

The property was placed into a trust by the deceased while he or she was still very much alive and assigned to a group of chosen trustees, although he or she retained control over their estate until their death. After death, the trustees would then dispose of the estate according to his or her wishes. Such agreements could be posthumously recorded by the trustees as a 'trust disposition and deed of settlement' (or more simply as a 'trust disposition and settlement') within the Register of Deeds of any competent court.

Extracts from such arrangements are included in the Wills database on ScotlandsPeople, found indexed with the abbreviation TD&S.

Types of Heir

One of the more confusing things that you will find named in both services and precepts of clare constat are the designations for various types of heirs that existed in law. The following are some of the more common.

Heir-at-Law (aka Heir-General and Heir of Line)

This was an heir inheriting via the rules of primogeniture. The heir was the deceased's eldest male son, or the second eldest son if the first was deceased, or third eldest if the second was also deceased, etc. If there were no sons, the heritage was equally split between all daughters; and if no daughters, it progressed to the deceased's younger male siblings, again in order of the eldest to the youngest.

Heir of Conquest

There were several ways that a person could obtain property: through inheritance, following an exchange with another landowner (known as 'excambion'), by gift, or through a purchase. The passing down to an heir of both types of acquisition after death was dealt with via the rules of primogeniture, so the eldest lawful son would inherit in the first instance, etc., or if he was dead then the second eldest, etc., as outlined above.

If there were no children, however, things became more interesting. In this case, any property held by the deceased that had been inherited by him would pass down to the next oldest sibling. However, any property that had been purchased in his lifetime – known in the jargon as having been obtained 'by conquest' – would actually go in the other direction, to an older brother or an uncle.

A simple rule governed the process when this happened: 'heritage descends, conquest ascends'. The person inheriting the conquest, whether a lawful son or an older sibling or uncle, was thereafter termed an 'heir of conquest'. This method of conveying conquest separately was abandoned after 1874.

Heir of Provision (or Destination)
This is an heir who becomes so because of express provisions made in a settlement in the deceased's will.

Heirs Portioners
This refers to the daughters of the deceased inheriting estate jointly if there were no male heirs, with each receiving an equal share. When one of the women subsequently died, her eldest son would succeed to her share, and from this point he too could be described as an heir portioner.

Heir of Tailzie
A landowner could maintain a form of control over the destination of the inheritance for several generations by 'entailing' it. A deed called a 'tailzie' or 'taillie' would be drawn up, through which he could lay down the particular lines of descent that he wished the estate to pass through. If the first family member listed was deceased by the time of the landowner's own death, it would pass to a second named individual (and his heirs), and if he had passed away then to a third and so on. As such, tailzies can be useful in identifying entire families, with the nomination of so many alternative lines. An heir who subsequently inherited because of such a provision was known as an 'heir of tailzie' (or 'of entail').

Often with a tailzie, if the line of inheritance should fall onto a daughter or other female member of the family, a condition would be set whereby she could only inherit the land if she first married somebody with the same surname as the creator of the tailzie, or somebody who would be willing to take on that name. In addition, that husband would also have to assume the set of Arms inherited by his wife, and in effect legally become a member of that family as if he had done so from birth. This would allow the identity of that family and, more importantly, the political weight of that family name, to remain undiminished in an area.

Such arrangements were recorded in a separate Register of Tailzies from 1688 and held at the NRS. For land to be freed from a tailzie or taillie an Act of Parliament was required, but from 1848 land could be 'disentailed' (freed from the conditions of a tailzie), the details of which are also included in the register.

Ultimus Haeres Records

Following the death of a person, if no will was left, and after a suitable period of advertising no claimant had stepped forward to inherit his or her estate (moveable and/or heritable), then the deceased's estate could be claimed in Scotland by the Queen's and Lord Treasurer's Remembrancer for the Crown (QLTR), as the ultimus haeres, or 'last heir'.

While the Crown is not obliged to honour any subsequent claim made on the estate after this, in practice it does so if the claim is deemed to be legitimate. Such claims are handled by the National Ultimus Haeres Unit in Hamilton, Lanarkshire (**www.qltr.gov.uk**). Claimants must provide proof of their relationship to the deceased, meaning that historic ultimus haeres records can be incredibly useful for genealogical purposes. Records are held at the NRS, catalogued within the Exchequer and Treasury records (under 'E').

In one interesting case I was asked to trace the relationship between two gentlemen, one having died in 1910, and the other seeking to claim from his estate two years later. The deceased had no lawful issue, and as such, his estate was believed to have fallen to the Crown as ultimus haeres. The ultimus haeres lists and accounts for the period in question (catalogued under E869) confirmed this to have happened in 1911.

I then called up the treasury report in which the case would have been mentioned, as sometimes genealogical evidence, including family tree charts, can be included. No such tree was to be found, but the report did note that the deceased's unclaimed estate had fallen to the Crown on 14 February 1911 and that his lands were due to be sold off in nine lots. After any debts incurred by the deceased were paid off, the rest of the proceeds were to go to the office of the King's and Lord Treasurer's Remembrancer (KLTR, the QLTR's contemporary equivalent).

My next task was to consult the relevant ultimus haeres 'procedure books' (catalogued under E851), which summarize developments concerning the administration of unclaimed estates that have fallen to the Crown. In this case I was fortunate to locate a five-page-long report summarizing written conversations held between the agents of the claimant and the KLTR office, which finally revealed some genealogical information. The documents asserted that the claimant was descended from the deceased's great-aunt, although no names were provided on his direct line back to her. Some genealogical records on the deceased's claimed ancestry were included, however, which led the KLTR office to become deeply unconvinced, not least because the claimant was maintaining that the deceased's grandfather had been aged just over 13 and a half years old when he married.

The ultimus haeres letter books for the period from 1910 to 1913, catalogued under E854, revealed that the genealogical problems causing the KLTR office grief were all too real, with the bride of the deceased's grandfather now stated to have been aged 24 when she married her 13 and a half-year-old husband. The KLTR office was having none of it, and was minded to reject the application, noting the relationship to be 'unsatisfactorily established'.

In this particular case, however, things then took an unexpected turn. Clearly frustrated with the KLTR's objections to the claim, the claimant decided to pursue a very separate strategy by having himself formally recognized as the deceased's heir through the services of heirs procedure (p.121). Against the KLTR's objections at the hearing, a jury at the sheriff court in Perth took a look at the family trees and other evidence placed before it and contented itself that the claimant did indeed have the right to be recognized as the deceased's heir-at-law, noting him to be his second cousin. This move by the claimant to have himself recognized by a court as the lawful heir instead of the KLTR office seems to have been enough to force the release of the assets held by the Crown, despite the KLTR office's deep apprehension.

As can be seen, such records can not only provide useful genealogical information in their own right, but in some instances a whole new epic story for the family history.

Chapter 8

LAW AND ORDER

In Chapter 2, the role of the kirk session within each parish was discussed, a body which would hear cases of breaches of church discipline. Among the offences that could be investigated and punished by the session were participation in irregular marriage, antenuptial fornication, profanity, disrespecting the Sabbath and defamation. If the decisions and punishments of the session were ignored by the guilty party, the session could call on the local justice of the peace (p.148) for support to help implement a sentence, or refer a case to the burgh court if within a burgh (p.145).

For more serious cases, however, and for actions that fell within certain specific judicial categories, there were other courts established by the state. In this chapter I will discuss the roles of these courts and the types of records that they generated.

Scots Law
Scots Law is an entirely different legal system to English Law. Although there has been some overlap and convergence since the union of 1707, there are many offences and legal terms that have no equivalent elsewhere in the British Isles. Thankfully there are many excellent legal dictionaries available online on Google Books and the Internet Archive which can be of great assistance in understanding the crimes and the processes to explore them. These include:

- Barclay, Hugh (1855), *A Digest of the Law of Scotland, with Special Reference to the Offices and Duties of a Justice of the Peace* (second edition)
- Bell, William (1838), *A Dictionary and Digest of the Law of Scotland*
- Blair, William (1834), *The Scottish Justices Manual; being an Alphabetical Compendium of the Powers and Duties of the Justices of the Peace within Scotland*.

Several courts have existed in Scotland since the medieval period which have historically administered justice on behalf of the Crown and which continue to do so. Most of their surviving records are held at the NRS or within local archives.

Sheriff Courts

In the medieval period the Crown provided justice for many criminal matters, such as theft or assault, through a corrupt system of local sheriff courts, overseen by sheriff-deputes who held their positions on a hereditary basis. Following the Heritable Jurisdictions (Scotland) Act of 1746, there were many changes implemented to the system; from this point onwards the country's sheriffs were all appointed, along with their deputies (sheriff-substitutes), to preside within a newly-restructured county-based sheriff court system. Their responsibilities in handling criminal cases were vast, while in the nineteenth century their remit was expanded further to handle certain civil matters such as small debts cases, testamentary matters, maritime cases and sequestrations (bankruptcies).

The most serious criminal cases, however, such as murder, rape, arson and robbery (known as the 'four pleas of the Crown'), in addition to cases of treason, were heard prior to 1672 by the country's 'justiciars', royal judges who operated judicial circuits known as 'ayres' on behalf of the Crown. The role of these justiciars and sheriffs was limited as much of the nation's land was held from the Crown by feudal landowners who also had rights to dispense justice on their territory through what were termed franchise courts (p.145).

The system changed in 1672, with the establishment of the High Court of Justiciary, Scotland's new supreme court, which travelled regularly on four circuits across the country, but which also heard cases within a permanent facility in Edinburgh (today also in Glasgow and Aberdeen).

Criminal trials held at the High Court from 1800 to 1994 can be searched for through the NRS catalogue, with precognitions or witness statements prepared by the Lord Advocate's Department catalogued under AD, and judicial process papers under JC. A useful NRS guide on High Court Criminal Trials is available online at **www.nrscotland.gov.uk/research/guides/high-court-criminal-trials**. At the time of writing, further High Court records from 1800 to 1916 are also being indexed by Scottish Indexes (p.5).

In addition to criminal cases, the sheriff courts maintained their own registers of deeds (p.109) and heard services of heirs cases (p.121), while throughout the nineteenth century, they took on responsibility for additional areas of civil jurisdiction, including small debts cases, sequestrations from 1839 (p.142), confirmation cases for inheritance (p.117), and Fatal Accident Inquiries from 1895 (p.136).

A detailed guide to the role of the sheriff courts and their records at the NRS, catalogued under SC, is available online at **www.nrscotland. gov.uk/research/guides/sheriff-court-records**

Privy Council

Just to complicate things, until 1708 it was also possible for some criminal cases and appeals to be heard by the Privy Council, a body which advised the monarch and was the equivalent of the Cabinet in today's Scottish Parliament. Its judicial role was curtailed with the creation of the Court of Session in 1532, while the Privy Council was itself abolished following the union in 1707, with the High Court becoming supreme.

A guide to the court and its holdings is available at **www.nrscotland. gov.uk/research/guides/privy-council-records**

Ardrossan Castle in Ayrshire, where the Privy Council met on 18 June 1546. For much of its existence, the Privy Council met in the Palace of Holyrood, but also convened at St Andrews and Stirling.

Criminal Prosecution

Among the crimes for which a person could be prosecuted were the following, some of which are still enforceable to this day:

Assault: this did not need to involve being physically struck by an opponent; for example, if someone pointed a gun at a person (even if unloaded), spat at an individual, or rode towards someone on a horse.

Bigamy: the act of marrying a second spouse while the first was still alive, something made a crime in Scots Law from 1551. Upon prosecution, the guilty offender could have his or her goods confiscated and be imprisoned. In a small number of aggravated cases transportation was the punishment.

Defamation: this was the wilful attempt to blacken the name of a person by calling into question their good name, character or credit.

Hamesucken: this was an assault of a person in their own house, where the aggressor has deliberately stepped into the property to do so. The crime is still prosecuted in Scotland to this day.

Housebreaking: the Scots term for burglary.

Poaching: in 1817, the Night Poaching Act (57 Geo. III c. 90) decreed that anyone caught poaching for game or rabbits at night with a weapon, or accompanying somebody with a weapon, was liable to seven years' transportation. A further Act in 1828 (9 Geo. IV c. 69) allowed for that sentence to be extended to fourteen years transportation if there were at least three poachers caught, and if one of them was armed.

Rape: unlawful sex without consent was a crime formerly punishable by death, although this was commuted to transportation in 1841.

Stouthrief: the theft of property from a building in the presence of its occupants.

Theft: this was the stealing of property for personal gain. The petty form of theft was known as 'pickery'.

A public prosecutor in Scotland was (and still is) known as a 'procurator fiscal', and could be appointed by a sheriff, a magistrate, or a justice of the peace in a quarter session (p.148). If a case went to trial then 'advocates' would be appointed to plead on behalf of both the accused and the defence. The accused was referred to as the 'pannel', and would have to 'compear', i.e. appear as the witness, before the court to be tried.

Note that when tried for criminal cases under Scots Law, people normally stood before a jury of fifteen jurors (this was also later introduced for civil cases in 1815), with a majority decision by the jury enough to carry a verdict. For a crime to have been committed, it had to have involved 'dole', or evil intent. There were three possible verdicts in a case: 'guilty' (historically this was previously given as fylit, culpable or convict), 'not guilty' (historically clenset, clean, acquit, or innocent) and 'not proven'. In a case found not proven, the accused was strongly presumed to have committed the crime, but there has not been enough evidence found to convict, meaning that he or she can walk away, albeit with a suspicion of guilt remaining over their heads.

It was not possible to be tried twice for the same crime under Scots Law until the passing of the Double Jeopardy (Scotland) Act in 2011.

Case Study: The Mount Stewart Murder

Under Scots Law, if a person has been killed through wrongful conduct but with no malice aforethought, the killing is referred to as one of 'culpable homicide' rather than the English legal term of 'manslaughter'. If there was a deliberate and unlawful attempt to end someone's life, however, the charge was that of 'murder'. Historically, there were many ways that one could be accused of the crime: for example, an old law from 1450 treated the importers of poison to the country as murderers, for which the sentence was execution.

The longest confirmed unsolved murder case by a modern Scottish police force, that is still technically an open investigation, is a story

that I know only too well. In the afternoon of 30 March 1866, my three-times great-grandmother Janet Rogers, née Henderson, was brutally clubbed to death with an axe in the kitchen of her brother William's home, Mount Stewart Farm, near Forgandenny, Perthshire. A year-long investigation into the crime concluded with a trial in April 1867 of the farm's ploughman, James Crichton, at the High Court circuit in Perth. After two days of deliberation the jury returned a verdict of non-proven, and Crichton walked away free.

The Mount Stewart Murder of 1866 remains Scotland's longest unsolved 'cold case' by a modern police force.

In researching the incident at the NRS, I first discovered the 'precognition papers', catalogued under AD14/67/170. These contained a series of witness statements, usually conducted without the subject being placed under oath, that were conducted in the immediate investigation (the 'precognition') of the murder. They were not admissible as evidence in the trial, but instead part of the initial documentation gathered by the fiscal to help prepare his case. It is worth noting that precognitions are closed to public access if less than seventy-five years old, and few survive before 1812. In this case, they not only included details relevant to the investigation, but also revealed all sorts of historical gems, such as the fact that my ancestor had a secret snuff habit that her husband was unaware of, her daughter Ann was almost blind, and that her husband James Rogers, my three-times great-grandfather, had been away from home for a few weeks prior to the incident, working on an estate near Dunkeld.

Another valuable source available was the collection of case papers (JC26/1867/20), also known as the 'process papers' or 'small papers'. These contained a range of extraordinary finds, such as an autopsy report on my ancestor, and a note written by my four-times great-uncle just an hour after he had found his sister's body, seeking help from the office of the procurator fiscal in nearby Perth. There were also minutes from the court proceedings (JC11/104) from the two days of the trial, and some architectural plans of the farm (RHP141081/1-2), drawn up the morning after the murder, which depicted where the body was found in the kitchen and included a sketch of the axe used as the murder weapon.

The newspaper coverage of the story across Britain, in addition to the local coverage in Perthshire, was extensive; I found several stories across the English press and even one account written in Welsh. Many of these stories were found at the A.K. Bell Library in Perth, with additional coverage available through the British Newspaper Archive (**www. britishnewspaperarchive.co.uk**). Perth and Kinross Archive (**www. culturepk.org.uk/archive-local-family-history**) was also extremely useful in my research in holding various police records (p.149).

Fatal Accident Enquiries

Following the implementation of the Fatal Accidents Inquiry (Scotland) Act 1895, a sheriff-led jury-based system was implemented to examine the cause of death for various industrial accidents. This Act was amended in 1906 to take into account some non-industrial-related sudden or suspicious deaths, although the jury component was eventually abandoned by a further reform in 1976.

Not all procurator fiscal or fatal accident enquiry records have survived, but a guide on how to locate those that have is available on the NRS website at **www.nrsscotland.gov.uk/research/guides/fatal-accident-inquiry-records**

Court of Session

When it came to matters of civil law the medieval sheriffs and their courts had some jurisdiction, but from 1532 cases could also be heard by the new superior Court of Session, established by James V and presided over by the Lord Chancellor of Scotland. In 1810 this court was subsequently divided into two, with an Outer House (a court of first instance) and Inner House (a court both of first instance and appeal). In 1815 a Jury Court was also created to allow trial by jury for civil matters for the first time, though this was absorbed into the Court of Session in 1830.

The Court of Session has overseen many civil actions, including issues such as debt recovery (p.138), divorce actions from 1830 to 1984, sequestrations (p.142), the appointment of guardians to oversee the estates of the sick or insane, and cases of defamation. It also has the most prominent series of registers of deeds (p.109), and could hear services of heirs cases (p.121).

The records of the court are held at the NRS and catalogued under CS. The archive offers a series of detailed research guides to help a user understand how to navigate through them at **www.nrsscotland.gov.uk/research/guides/court-of-session-records**

For most cases after 1660 you will be searching for the 'processes', or papers, which can come in two forms: 'extracted processes' where a 'decreet' by the Lords of Council and Session has been extracted as part of the process to issue a warrant for the action decreed (and recorded within the Register of Acts and Decreets), or 'unextracted processes' where no such extraction was made but where court papers from a particular case may still exist. You will unlikely know whether there are extracted or unextracted papers for a case of interest, and whether you know the names of the defenders and pursuers can also affect how you might locate such records. There are further differences in the research approach for cases that occurred prior to 1660, for which you will need to consult either the series of general minute books or particular minute books.

Many Court of Session cases are indexed on the NRS catalogue and in card indexes available onsite. Some select cases from the court have also been published, with several volumes accessible online via Google Books and the Internet Archive.

Debt

One of the biggest areas of litigation for which the Court of Session heard cases was that of debt. There were many ways that people could find themselves in financial straits, with some simply borrowing money and then forgetting to carry out the paying back part; others would succumb to falling wages and increasing inflation; while many also found themselves the victims of business investments that failed to realize their potential.

For some, entire estates could be lost, with land having previously been offered as a surety to back up a loan or 'wadset' (the Scots term for a mortgage). Such loans in security (called 'bonds') could be recorded in the sasines registers (p.104) or registers of deeds (p.109).

Prior to 1838, if a person failed to pay his or her debts, they could be punished quite harshly with imprisonment and the seizure of assets. The process for civil debt recovery was for the creditor, the person to whom the money was owed, to first demand payment of the outstanding debt, within six months of the due date, through a document called a 'protest'; this essentially warned the debtor to pay up or else. If the creditor still had no joy following this, he or she could register the protest with any competent court to pursue the debt further with its support. This would then form the warrant for a 'letter of horning', which laid out the full terms of the agreement and the money still outstanding, with an instruction for the debt to be paid up immediately on pain of the debtor being declared a 'rebel' (having 'rebelled' against the Sovereign's demands to pay up).

Any of the lower courts could be petitioned for this, but the authority had to be granted ultimately by the Court of Session as such demands for repayment were to be made in the Sovereign's name. Included with the letter of horning was a warrant to 'poind' (pronounced 'pind') the debtor's moveable assets in case of non-payment; in other words, to seize any money, assets or valuables that were owned by the offender (excluding the house or any land), which could then be sold to recoup the costs.

The letter of horning would be read out publicly by a messenger-at-arms at a town's market cross, after blowing a horn three times in advance, giving rise to the expression of a debtor being 'put to the horn'. Because they had disobeyed the authority of the Crown, such debtors were proclaimed as rebels. Fifteen days were given for the debt to be paid back in full (forty if in Orkney or Shetland), unless some other specific duration was mentioned in the document. If the debtor failed to pay back what was owed in the allotted period, the Crown then issued a 'letter of caption', authorizing the messenger-at-arms to take the debtor into custody, at which point his or her estate was then poinded.

There were other ways that debtors could be punished by the courts. In addition to their moveable assets being poinded, any heritable property could be prevented from being sold off through the grant of a legal document in favour of the creditor called an 'inhibition'. Prior to 1672, a debtor's heritable rights to a property could also be sold off against his or her will through a process called 'apprising'. This required the debtor to sell his or her holdings within fifteen days to satisfy the debt, by sheriff's order. If he or she failed to do so, the entire property would be transferred to the creditor without the debtor's consent, though there was a limited time period of seven years after this in which the debtor could redeem the property if the debt was repaid along with other legal costs.

This system was replaced by a process called 'adjudication', handled by the Court of Session, whereby the court would value the debtor's property and transfer only a determined part of it to the creditor. Again, the debtor could redeem the property after, but within the shorter period of five years, as opposed to seven.

Case Study: Matthew Campbell of Waterhaughs

In 1683, the lands of Ayrshire landowner Matthew Campbell of Waterhaughs were declared forfeit during the reign of Charles II. Although later finding favour again with the Crown in 1689, Campbell had amassed a substantial series of debts in the interim, and over many years prior, from which he was never to recover.

In February 1693 Campbell had failed to pay back to one of his creditors, David Patterson, a sum of £433 6s 8d Scots which he had borrowed a year earlier. On 11 July 1693 he received a demand for the money to be paid back within six days 'under pain of rebellion and putting of him to our horn'. The demand was ignored; therefore a letter of horning was drawn up against him by John Cockburne, sheriff clerk of Ayr. Campbell was detained and subsequently denounced at the market cross, where it was publicly proclaimed that he had

> most contemptuously disobeyed the command & charge given to
> him in manner fors[ai]d. Therefore upon the ffyfth day of August...
> I David Patterson messinger past to the mercat cross of Air head
> burgh of the sherriffdom yrof and yrat after the crying of three
> seall oyez open proclaimen & publick overreading of the sds...
> letters I Duly Law[fu]lly and orderly den[o]unced the s[ai]d Mr

Mathew Campbell there majestie's Rebell and putt him to there highnes horne by three blasts of ane horn as use is And ordaines all his moveable goods and geir to be escheat and brought to there majesties use for his contemptione and disobedience.

(Court of Session, Scotland. Creditors of Campbell, of Watterhaugh vs Creditors Campbell, of Waterhaugh: Decreet of Ranking of Creditors (part only) CS138/1261. National Records of Scotland)

In the same year, a separate decreet of horning and poinding was also initiated against Campbell by an Elizabeth Neilson, the document being dated 10 March 1693 and executed on 18 November 1693, concerning a much larger debt accrued since 1675. As Campbell's lands had been forfeited for part of this duration, he asked the Court of Session on 3 January 1694 to overturn the charge of horning. The Lords considered the case and agreed that his liabilities for the period in which he was forfeit could be 'superseded'; in other words the payment for this could be postponed, although they noted that the charge of horning had been warrantable for the amount preceding the forfeiture.

On the basis of this judgement, some six months later Elizabeth Neilson had a 'decree of suspension' granted on 21 July 1694 against Campbell for income expected from 1675 to 1690, totalled at £1,602 6s 8d Scots. Instead, letters were executed against him for just eleven of those years from 1675 to 1683 (preceding his forfeiture) and from 1689 to 1690 (following his restitution). The reduced total now owed was valued at £1,122 4s Scots, plus a further reduced payment of £146 13s 4d for the remaining period during his forfeiture.

By the end of the following year, 1695, Campbell had still not repaid his debt and was imprisoned. Once again he turned to the Court of Session for help. He took a further action against Neilson on the basis that a law previously passed for people in his position, 'the 16th Act of Parliament 1695, suspending all personal execution against persons in his circumstances till Whitsunday 1696' rendered him immune from imprisonment until then. The Lords ruled against him.

Campbell's luck ran from bad to worse, with the unlucky laird losing £100 through the Darien Scheme of 1696. For the remainder of his life he was caught up in continual litigation against many creditors, being eventually forced by relatives to sell his estate as a bankrupt in 1708. On 9 August, just days before the roup (auction) was due to commence, Campbell instead paid the piper and passed away.

Bankruptcy

For entrepreneurs within Scottish society, there was no greater shame than for a business to fail. If a business person became insolvent, the law historically found little sympathy for the bankrupt and every sympathy for the creditors.

Prior to 1771, the main method for a business person to try to discharge a debt and to avoid imprisonment for bankruptcy was to apply for 'cessio bonorum'. Initially heard only at the Court of Session, but from 1836 also by sheriff courts, the process allowed a debtor to appear before his creditors to explain the circumstances that had led them towards bankruptcy and try to prove that the failure had been caused by misfortune as opposed to mismanagement or fraud. Prior to a hearing it was possible for the applicant to be arrested and imprisoned.

If the application got as far as the court, and the debtor's creditors were satisfied that misfortune had indeed been the cause, the debtor could be freed from the threat of imprisonment, and a 'disposition omnium bonorum' granted in favour of the creditors through an appointed trustee; this essentially conveyed all the debtor's remaining assets to them to satisfy the debt. A person who withheld any part of his estate from his or her creditors was not entitled to go through the cessio process, and could be imprisoned until everything owned was declared.

Once the cessio was granted the debtor was further protected from any subsequent arrests. However, if the debtor's goods, once sold, did not realize enough money to pay off the creditors, they were perfectly entitled to pursue the debtor for any further acquisitions or earnings he might make until the debt was paid off. In such a case the creditors could again take the debtor to court until the full debt was finally repaid.

William Bell's *A Dictionary and Digest of the Law of Scotland* notes that the debtor only had limited rights up to this point:

> In surrendering to his creditors either new acquisitions or the property formerly belonging to him, the debtor is not entitled to retain anything but his work tools, properly so called... and where the debtor has a fixed salary, it is settled that he must give up all that exceeds a proper aliment. Thus clergymen have been held bound to give up part of their stipend, and officers in the army a proportion of their half-pay.

> (Bell, William (1838), *A Dictionary and Digest of the Law of Scotland*. Edinburgh: John Anderson, Royal Exchange, p.138.)

If your ancestor applied for cessio bonorum, a useful starting-point is to consult the *Edinburgh Gazette* via **www.thegazette.co.uk**. From 1836 local sheriffs had to publish a notice in the *Gazette* to compel creditors to step forward within thirty days. The following is a typical example from 1894:

> A PETITION for Cessio, under the Cessio Acts, has been presented to the Sheriff of Perthshire at Perth, by JOSEPH HALL, Clematis Villa, Friar Street, Craigie, Perth; and the Sheriff Substitute has ordained the said Joseph Hall to appear for public Examination within the Sheriff Court House, County Buildings, Perth, upon the 11th day of May next, at two o'clock afternoon, at which Diet all his Creditors are required to attend.
>
> JOHN A. STEWART, Solicitor
> 42 Tay Street, Perth
> Agent for Petitioner
>
> Perth, 26th April 1894.
>
> (Unknown. 1894. A Petition for Cessio. *Edinburgh Gazette*, Issue 10565, p.503, 27 April.)

From the late eighteenth century an alternative to cessio bonorum was the process known as 'sequestration'. If a person became bankrupt there were two ways that sequestration of their assets could be awarded. The first was at the instance of the bankrupt with the agreement of one of the creditors. The other was without the bankrupt's agreement, but at the instance of a creditor who was owed at least £100 (or two creditors owed £150, or three creditors owed £200, etc.). In such a case a trustee elected by the creditors was formally appointed by the Court of Session to administer the estate of the bankrupt, and to dispose of its assets until all the debts were paid off. As part of his duties the trustee had to list the creditors in order of priority of payment, which could sometimes lead to legal proceedings between creditors also (arguing over who had priority), all under the watchful eye of the court.

The full debt did not always have to be paid off if the creditors accepted a 'composition' from the debtor; this was a proportion of the debt owed, which if accepted by both the court and the creditors, could curtail the length of time of the sequestration process. As with cessio, cases of sequestration are also to be found listed within the *Edinburgh Gazette*.

The NRS has a considerable number of records concerning bankruptcy. Sequestration cases from 1838 onwards are recorded in three main series of processes under CS280, CS318 and CS319; all have been indexed on the archive's online catalogue, but for cases prior to this you may need to do a little more digging at the facility itself. A research guide for the relevant Court of Session holdings is accessible through the archive at **www.nrscotland.gov.uk/research/research-guides/research-guides-a-z/ court-of-session-records/sequestrations**

Case Study: John Brownlie MacFarlane

It is always worth trying to examine sequestration papers if possible, as they can reveal a great deal of additional detail about the bankrupt both prior to the sequestration and after. A useful example of this lies with the sequestration of my two-times great-grandfather's assets in the late nineteenth century.

John Brownlee MacFarlane was a Glasgow-born tailor and clothier who had worked initially in Inverness for his father-in-law David MacGillivray before relocating to Nairn in 1870 to set up his own business. Some eight years later trade had taken a turn for the worse and in August 1878 John petitioned the court to have his estate sequestrated, with the agreement of a draper and creditor called Charles Bain Mackintosh. Notices were duly published in the *Edinburgh Gazette*, the *Inverness Courier* and the *Inverness Advertiser*. At a creditors' meeting Mackintosh was appointed as trustee to oversee the process.

Once the value of John's assets was totalled and deductions made for him to pay his rent, it was discovered that he had only £21 6s to pay off debts amounting to £158 17s 6d, not including additional court costs. A composition was offered by John of payment of a shilling per pound owed, which was accepted by his creditors, but soon the tailor had problems paying even this. A letter from Mackintosh in 1882 includes a revised valuation of John's assets, which notes that after deductions for rents and taxes he had a

> probable balance of £8 6s to meet £158 of ordinary debts due by the Bankrupt, besides the expenses of Sequestration which can never be paid looking to the value of the estate and the poor circumstances of the Bankrupt whose health is also broken down.

> (Court of Session: Sequestration Processes, Special Transmission. 1911. John Brownlee McFarlane, Nairn, tailor and clothier. CS319/1911/2202. National Records of Scotland)

Thankfully John's health eventually returned to him in good order, and he was subsequently discharged from the debt.

An interesting find from this was the name of the trustee, Charles Bain Mackintosh. In 1873 John and his wife Ann had a son called Charles Mackintosh MacFarlane. It is possible that John's son was named after the Nairn-based draper, which may imply that he was a family friend.

Commissary Courts

The commissary courts were a remnant of the pre-Reformation era, having previously existed as the consistorial (diocesan) courts of the Roman Catholic Church, with the principal court in Edinburgh. From 1564 they were reconstituted as a civil court, with jurisdictions over local

The grave of John Brownlie MacFarlane, the author's great-great-grandfather, at Tomnahurich Cemetery, Inverness.

'commissariots' (based on the former Catholic dioceses), and dealing primarily with confirmation (p.117) matters, marriage cases, illegitimacy issues and tutelage. The courts could also hear debt cases (up to £40 Scots) and defamation cases, and until 1809 they also maintained their own Registers of Deeds. Any appeals to their judgements were usually heard by the Court of Session. The inferior Commissary Courts were eventually abolished in 1823, and their responsibilities transferred to the sheriff courts; by 1836 Edinburgh Commissary Court had also been abolished.

The records for testaments granted through the courts are available on ScotlandsPeople (p.2), although not all cases completed the confirmation process, with the court papers containing many additional cases. In addition to confirmation and testamentary materials, the NRS also holds act and diet books, decrees, processes, court proceedings, petitions, tutorial and curatorial papers, deeds and protests, and bonds and acts of caution, as detailed in its online guide at **www.nrscotland.gov.uk/research/guides/commissary-court-records**

Cases concerning marriage, divorce and separation could only be heard by Edinburgh Commissary Court, for which a register was kept from

1684 to 1830. Before 1560 a couple could be separated in Scotland because of adultery, but the participants could not remarry. The annulment of a marriage was possible, however, due to nonage, insanity, impotency or bigamy. In 1567 a breach of the laws surrounding consanguinity was added as a further ground for annulment, and in 1573 divorce could be granted for desertion if the husband had abandoned his wife for four years or more.

A pursuer in a case concerning adultery had to appear before the court and swear an 'oath of calumny', stating his or her belief in their spouse's guilt and that there was no collusion to fraudulently seek a divorce. If the court believed the pursuer's story, the spouse was effectively declared 'legally dead', and the pursuer granted the share of assets that would have been granted upon a natural death of his or her spouse.

As the influence of the church began to wane in society, cases of divorces in the cities leaped dramatically in the cities by the mid-eighteenth century. A superb account detailing many Edinburgh Commissary Court divorce cases is *Alienated Affections: The Scottish Experience of Divorce and Separation, 1684–1830* by Leah Leneman (Edinburgh University Press, 1998).

The court was also asked to judge if contracted marriages were valid through 'declarators of marriage', gathering evidence in various forms, including written promises and witnessed 'beddings'. If the marriage was proved, the defender would have to pay alimony, and any children born to them were considered legitimate. Conversely, a 'declarator of freedom' could also be pursued to confirm that an alleged marriage had never been contracted.

If a woman believing herself to be married lost her case, she could still pursue her perceived 'spouse' for seduction, although any children born to her from her partner would be deemed illegitimate. A further book from Leah Leneman, *Promises, Promises: Marriage Litigation in Scotland 1698–1830* (NMS Enterprises, 2003), examines cases in Edinburgh Commissary Court concerning the validity of irregular marriages, including those by promise subsequente copula (p.23).

Franchise and Burgh Courts

While the Crown held ultimate authority over civil and criminal matters, many feudal landholders also held judicial responsibilities over their estates.

In certain areas of Scotland known as 'baronies', these landowners could prosecute virtually any crime or civil offence on their patch, holding powers over 'pit and gallows, sake and soke, toll, team and infangthief', though this excluded cases concerning the four pleas of the Crown (p.132) and treason. Within their judicial competence the feudal barons held the right to dispense capital punishment, the traditional means of execution usually being to drown women in a pit (often called a 'murder hole'), and to hang men from a gibbet. Larger feudal jurisdictions called 'regalities', of which there were only a handful, had even stronger quasi-regal powers, and could also dispense punishment for the pleas of the Crown. Further courts included 'bailiery courts' and 'stewartry courts'.

The authority of these 'franchise courts', as they were termed, had declined markedly by the sixteenth century, although many still exercised rights until their eventual abolition via the Heritable Jurisdictions (Scotland) Act of 1746. This piece of legislation, which followed Bonnie Prince Charlie's failed Jacobite rebellion, was designed both to remove the ability of clan chiefs to raise armies, but also to transfer all judicial functions from feudal landholders to the Crown 'for rendering the Union of the Two Kingdoms more complete', the union with England having been previously contracted in 1707.

Surviving franchise court records may be found within estate papers held at the NRS, in local archives or within private collections. To find those in a local archive, check the SCAN catalogue or the archive's own dedicated online catalogue, if it has one. Private holdings, if catalogued, may be accessible via the NRAS. A more detailed examination of the franchise courts is discussed by Alexander Grant in his essay *Franchises North of the Border: Baronies and Regalities in Medieval Scotland*, available online at **https://eprints.lancs.ac.uk/633/1/Grant_Franchises.pdf**

Working alongside the franchise courts were the courts of the royal burghs, areas erected with exclusive privileges for trading, and the forerunners of many modern towns and cities. Burgh courts had powers for minor civil and criminal cases within their jurisdiction, such as civil disputes over payments owed, assault or breach of the peace. Cases could also be referred to them by kirk sessions to help enforce moral discipline. Punishments imposed by them could include imprisonment, a public flogging or even banishment from the burgh.

For the courts of the royal burghs, a small number are held at the NRS, catalogued with the prefix 'B', but many more are held in local archives across the country (see above). In most cases the records are usually not indexed. To give an example of the wide areas over which burgh courts held responsibility, as well as an indication of the records that may have survived, Glasgow City Archives notes the following holdings for the burgh of Glasgow and the nearby smaller burgh of Rutherglen:

Glasgow Burgh Courts:
Services of Heirs, 1625–1866
Justices of Peace Court, 1663–1680
Register of Deeds, 1625–1973 (also printed indexes for the rest of
Scotland, 1665–1683)
Small Debt Court, 1773–1817
Licensing Court, 1779–1977
Criminal Court, 1802–1950
Police Courts, 1805–1875
Central Police Court, 1906 (final sitting)

Rutherglen Burgh Courts:
Court, 1619–1975
Service of Heirs, 1794–1860
Registers of Deeds, 1628–1736

(Family History at the Mitchell, Courts guide, Glasgow, **www.
glasgowfamilyhistory.org.uk/ExploreRecords/Pages/Courts.aspx**,
accessed 23 April 2019.)

Trade Incorporations

Prior to the fifteenth century, tradesmen working in the country's royal
burghs had to be members of its merchant guild. On 12 March 1425 an
Act of Parliament was passed declaring that

> it is ordanyt that in ilk toune of the realme of ilk sindry craft oysit
> therin thar be chosing a vyse mane of that craft be the layff of that
> craft and the consall of the offysaris of the toune, the quhilk sall be
> haldin dekin and mastir our the layff for the tyme till hym assignyt
> till assay and govern all verkis that beys mayd be the verkmen of
> his craft, sua that the kyngis legis be nocht defraudyt in tym to cum
> as thai have bene in tym bygane throu untrew men of craftis.

(The Records of the Parliaments of Scotland to 1707, 1425/3/18.
www.rps.ac.uk. Date accessed: 24 April 2019.)

This paved the way for the creation of deacons and masters to lead
trade incorporations within Scotland, designed to protect the rights
of masons, weavers, hammermen, glovers, skinners, bakers and other
skilled craftsmen.

Upon completion of an apprenticeship, craftsmen had to become
'freemen' or 'burgesses' of their relevant 'callings' to operate within
a burgh. They could obtain their 'freedom' by marrying a freeman's

daughter, by completing an apprenticeship with a freeman, inheriting the right from their freeman father, or by purchase. This not only allowed them to trade freely and to purchase property there, but also granted them the right to vote in their incorporation's elections, as well as those of the burgh council.

The trade incorporations and merchant guilds maintained strict disciplinary structures. Among the court records of the Weavers Incorporation of Perth, for example, now held at Perth and Kinross Archives, is the following entry:

P[er]th the 10 Oct[obe]r 1705
Whilk Day the Generall meiting of the weavers of perth convened all in ane voice Unlaus and ffeynes Patrick Smith in five pounds and ordaines him to goe to prisone until pay[men]t because his wife abeused the pr[esen]tt deicon yrunto he is liable conforme to act of the court.

(Weavers Incorporation of Perth. Minute book 1701–1753. Perth and Kinross Archives)

A lesson was clearly not learned, with Patrick once again returning to prison for virtually the same offence after a subsequent court hearing on 19 February 1709, after 'Jannet Mackie his spouse Intruded herself in the Deacons company and without any ground of offence Did harrass and abuse him in a publick company', with the record this time giving us the courtesy of her name.

Justices of the Peace
The role of the justice of the peace pre-dates the seventeenth century, but the position was formally regulated in 1661 during the first Parliament of Charles II.

Justices were meant to meet four times a year at quarter session courts to hear minor cases, although the frequency varied from county to county. Cases heard included irregular marriages (p.46), riots, breach of the peace, minor assault, debt, begging and vagrancy, the vandalism of highways, drunkenness and profanity on the Sabbath. Justices also had the power to regulate labourers' wages (repealed in 1813) and to keep order in times of plague.

Justices were volunteers, given only a basic expenses allowance, and struggled to compete with the jurisdiction of the local sheriffs. However, their role did become more important following the union in 1707, when they were given equivalent powers to their English counterparts on issues of customs and excise. Their role often overlapped with the jurisdictions of the kirk sessions, occasionally causing friction at a local level.

Records are held at the NRS and at various local archives, with a guide to their location available at **www.nrscotland.gov.uk/research/guides/justices-of-the-peace-records**

Admiralty Court

The Admiralty Court held sway from 1557 to 1830 over maritime affairs on the high seas or in Scottish harbours, including criminal cases. They are catalogued under AC at the NRS.

J.D. Ford's *A Guide to the Procedure of the Admiralty Court* was published in the Scottish Record Association's Scottish Archives journal, Vol. 18, in 2012 and can be read online at **www.scottishrecordsassociation.org/Scottish%20Archives%2018.web.9%20Ford.pdf**

Court of the Lord Lyon

The Court of the Lord Lyon (p.3), led by the Lord Lyon King of Arms, deals with all issues concerning the law of Arms, i.e. heraldry, with the illegal use of someone's Arms treated as if it is theft. It should be noted that there is no such thing as a 'family Coat of Arms'; any set of Arms is the heritable property of one person only (p.120). The court still operates in Edinburgh and has its own procurator fiscal (p.134), with the Lord Lyon as the sitting judge. In addition to adjudication on all matters armorial, the court is also responsible for Grants of Arms in Scotland.

The official record of all Scottish coats of Arms is the *Public Register of All Arms and Bearings in Scotland*. First established in 1672, it contains written blazons (descriptions of Arms) and in some cases a brief genealogy. From 1804, Volume 2 depicts blazons accompanied by hand-painted depictions of the Arms granted and a brief summary of the genealogies of the petitioners if recorded when the application was made. This may go back a mere generation or two, or considerably further if an ancestor was also 'armigerous', i.e. entitled to the original, undifferenced design of a coat of Arms. Entries from the register up to 1916 have been digitized and made available to view on ScotlandsPeople.

For enquiries about records beyond 1916, and for other family trees and genealogical resources held within its possession, contact the Court of the Lord Lyon at H.M. New Register House, Edinburgh EH1 3YT.

Police and Prison Records

Police archive collections containing arrest books, charge books and letter books are always worth consulting at the relevant local authority

The regulation of heraldry in Scotland falls to the Court of the Lord Lyon.

archive. In the case of the Mount Stewart Murder (p.135), the arrest book for Perthshire Constabulary was found at Perth and Kinross Archive and noted that James Crichton, the labourer accused of the killing, was aged 40 and was 5ft 6in in height. Both the arrest book and the charge book were also updated after the trial to note that Crichton's alleged guilt had been found non-proven.

Police correspondence can also be useful to find out about ancestors who, although not prosecuted, still made contact with the forces concerned for a variety of reasons. These could include being warned about potential misdemeanours, those making complaints warranting investigation, or those who simply fell foul of the law for more trifling reasons. A good example lies in an incident from 1866, for which the Perthshire chief constable, George Gordon, wrote the following brief summary in the force's letter book:

Perth 3rd September 1866

Upon examining Sergeant Allan why the woman Elizabeth McMillan or McKay was so long detained in the cells at Aberfeldy – two days – he stated that he was sent for to the Breadalbane Hotel, the woman – a vagrant – was there drunk and incapable. She was lying in the Lobby and he had to get her conveyed to the Lockup in a wheelbarrow. This was about 2pm on Monday – and he relieved her at 10 o'clock am on Tuesday when sober on her promising to leave the village which she did.

(Perthshire Constabulary papers. Letter Book 1862–67. POL 1/5/3. Perth and Kinross Archives)

Another interesting example from the same register describes a spat with a local justice of the peace, who granted licences to two named publicans for selling excisable liquor at Alyth market. The chief constable wrote to the publicans concerned, James Simpson and David Young, both of Forfar, that if they proceeded with their sales they would be prosecuted under the Public Houses Act.

For criminals successfully convicted by the courts, the NRS holds prison registers for many areas of the country from the early- to mid-nineteenth century. A breakdown of such holdings is available at **www.nrscotland. gov.uk/research/guides/crime-and-criminals**. Most are indexed under HH21, and have been digitized and made available for consultation on its Virtual Volumes computer system.

Transportation

A common punishment of the eighteenth and nineteenth centuries, often for petty crime as much as for more serious transgressions, was transportation. In the aftermath of the mid-seventeenth-century Civil War in Britain, many Scots, along with Irish and Welsh royalists, were banished by Cromwell's protectorate to Barbados after being found guilty of high treason, a fate later also endured by Jacobites after their failed rebellions (p.91).

The first formal Transportation Act was in 1718, with the American colonies the main destination until the American Revolutionary War of the late 1770s. Following the secession of the new United States from British rule, Britain had to look elsewhere to banish its criminals, with the first convicts making their way to Australia in 1787. Sentences varied from seven years' to fourteen years' banishment, but in truth most who were transported remained in their new-found homes upon release.

In addition to many trial papers, the NRS also has several transportation papers for the period from 1653 to 1853 within its High Court records, catalogued under JC41, and transportation registers on microfilm for the period covering 1787 to 1870, catalogued under RH4/160/1-7.

Many records concerning those transported can also be found on Ancestry (**www.ancestry.co.uk**) and TheGenealogist (**www.thegenealogist.co.uk**).

Capital Punishment

Prior to the reigns of William IV and Victoria, various crimes warranted the death penalty, with some of the more unusual including returning from transportation, letter-stealing, sacrilege and forgery. Scotland had far fewer capital offences than England and Wales, which by 1834 had some 300 offences punishable by death, although many of these were commuted to transportation. By comparison, in the same year Scotland had less than thirty capital offences, reduced to just three by 1887 via the Criminal Procedure (Scotland) Act, these being murder, attempted murder and treason.

Capital punishment remained on the UK's statute books until 1965. Between 1800 and 1868, the year when the last public hanging occurred in Scotland, some 273 people were executed in this manner. The majority of the executions, some 125 cases, were for murder, followed by 55 felons killed by the state for housebreaking.

The stories of some of the most notable executions in Britain during the eighteenth and nineteenth centuries are available via the Capital Punishment site at www.capitalpunishmentuk.org. *The Scots Black Kalendar: Scottish Crime and Punishment* by Thomas Tod (Lang Syne Publishers, 1985) is a useful publication summarizing a century's worth of executions from the nineteenth century. The Black Sheep Ancestors site at **www.blacksheepancestors.com/uk** is another useful port of call.

BIBLIOGRAPHY/FURTHER READING

Anon, *The Parishes, Registers and Registrars of Scotland* (New Edition) (Oxford: The Scottish Association of Family History Societies, 2010)

Baptie, Diane, *Parish Registers in the Kirk Session Records of the Church of Scotland* (Aberdeen: The Scottish Association of Family History Societies, 2004)

Baptie, Diane, *Registers of the Secession Churches of Scotland* (Aberdeen: The Scottish Association of Family History Societies, 2000)

Bigwood, Rosemary, *The Scottish Family Tree Detective* (Manchester: Manchester University Press, 2006)

Bissett-Smith, G.T., *Vital Registration: A Manual of the Law and Practice Concerning the Registration of Births, Marriages and Deaths* (Edinburgh: W. Green and Sons, 1907)

Brown, Callum G., *Religion and Society in Scotland since 1707* (Edinburgh: Edinburgh University Press, 1997)

Clapton, Gary, *Relatively Clear: A Search for Adopted People in Scotland* (Edinburgh: Birthlink, 2009)

Clarke, Tristram, *Tracing Your Scottish Ancestors – The Official Guide* (6th edition) (Edinburgh, Birlinn Ltd, 2011)

Dobson, David, *Scottish Catholics at Home and Abroad 1680–1780* (Baltimore: Clearfield, 2010)

Gibb, Andrew Dewar, *Student's Glossary of Scottish Legal Terms* (Edinburgh: W. Green & Son Ltd, 1946)

Gibson, Jeremy and Medlycott, Mervyn, *Local Census Listings 1522–1930: Holdings in the British Isles* (Bury: FFHS, 2001)

Gibson, Jeremy, *Electoral Registers 1832–1948 and Burgess Rolls* (Bury: The Family History Partnership, 2008)

Gouldesbrough, Peter, *Formulary of Old Scots Documents (Edinburgh: The Stair Society, 1985)*

Hamilton-Edward, Gerald, *In Search of Scottish Ancestry* (Chichester: Phillimore & Co. Ltd, 1986)

Innes, Sir Thomas of Learney, *Scots Heraldry* (Edinburgh: Oliver & Boyd, 1956)

Kopittke, Rosemary, *ScotlandsPeople: The Place to Launch Your Scottish Research* (Adelaide: Unlock the Past, 2012)

Leneman, Leah, *Promises, Promises: Marriage, Litigation in Scotland 1698–1830* (Edinburgh: NMS Enterprises Limited, 2003)

Leneman, Leah, *Alienated Affections: The Scottish Experience of Divorce and Separation, 1684–1830* (Edinburgh: Edinburgh University Press, 1998)

Menzies, A., Mitford, J. and Hunter, J., *Conveyancing According to the Law of Scotland: Being the Edited Lectures of the Late Allan Menzies* (Edinburgh: Bell and Bradfute, 1863. Available online at Google Books)

Murray, James, *Life in Scotland a Hundred Years Ago as reflected in the Old Statistical Account of Scotland 1791–1799* (Paisley: Alexander Gardner, 1900)

Nisbet, Kenneth, *The Register of Corrected Entries and Its Use for Family History* (Edinburgh: Scottish Genealogy Society, 2013)

Paton, Chris, *Tracing Your Family History on the Internet* (2nd edition) (Barnsley: Pen & Sword Family History, 2014)

Paton, Chris, *The Mount Stewart Murder: A Re-examination of the UK's Oldest Unsolved Murder Case* (Stroud: The History Press, 2012)

Paton, David, *The Clergy and the Clearances: The Church and the Highland Crisis 1790–1850* (Edinburgh: John Donald, 2006)

Penny, George, *Traditions of Perth* (Perth: Messrs Dewar, Sidey, Morison, Peat and Drummond, 1836)

Prebble, John, *Culloden* (London: Pimlico, 2002)

Prebble, John, *The Highland Clearances* (London: Penguin Books, 1982)

Scottish Records Society, *Scottish Handwriting 1500–1700: A Self-Help Pack* (Edinburgh: Scottish Record Office, 1994)

Seafield, Lily, *Scottish Witches* (New Lanark: Waverley Press, 2009)

Simpson, Grant, *Scottish Handwriting 1150–1650: An Introduction to the Reading of Documents* (Edinburgh: John Donald Short Run Press, 2009)

Sinclair, Cecil, *Jock Tamson's Bairns: A History of the Records of the General Register Office for Scotland* (Edinburgh: General Register Office for Scotland, 2000)

Smout, T.C., *A Century of the Scottish People 1830–1950* (London: Fontana Press, 1997)

Smout, T.C., *A History of the Scottish People 1560–1830* (London: Fontana Press, 1998)

Steel, D.J., *National Index of Parish Registers Volume XII: Sources for Scottish Genealogy and Family History* (Chichester: Phillimore and Co. Ltd, 1970)

Watts, Christopher T. and Michael J., *My Ancestor Was a Merchant Seaman* (London: Society of Genealogists, 2002)

Wenzerul, Rosemary, *Jewish Ancestors? A Guide to Jewish Genealogy in the United Kingdom* (Revised 2011) (London: JGSGB Publications, 2011)

Wightman, Andy, *The Poor Had No Lawyers: Who Owns Scotland (And How They Got It)*, new edition (Edinburgh: Birlinn Ltd, 2013)

Wills, Virginia, *Reports on the Annexed Estates 1755–1769* (Edinburgh: HMSO, 1973)

INDEX